Learning by Doing

A Guide to Teaching and Learning Methods

GRAHAM GIBBS

© FEU 1988   ISBN 1 85338 071 7

Preface

The guide has itself been developed through experiential methods. Many of the methods described have been tried out in action research projects in a wide range of contexts. The members of the project team used experiential learning theory to plan experiential learning sessions, carried out these teaching and training sesions and then held de-briefings in which they reflected on their experiences in these sessions. More formal evaluation of methods has also been undertaken, using interviews and questionnaires. We have been lucky enough to be allowed to see how others use experiential learning methods on their courses and experienced teachers have given us detailed descriptions of their methods. We believe that the guide offers a cornucopia of ideas for implementing experiential learning and we are confident that you will find things which you can try out in your own teaching and training.

We would like to thank the following people for their help, co-operation and ideas in the preparation of this guide:

John Alexander, John Covell, John Cowan, Trevor Habeshaw, David Jaques, Tony Kelly, Paula McGee.

The 'Learning Through Doing' project team:

Bob Farmer
Project leader
Head, Educational Development Unit, Birmingham Polytechnic

Diana Eastcott
Senior Lecturer, Educational Development Unit, Birmingham Polytechnic

Graham Gibbs
Principal Lecturer, Educational Methods Unit, Oxford Polytechnic, and consultant to the project

Contents

Foreword

The relationship between theory and its practical applications has been at the top of the education and training agenda for a decade or so. Traditionally, teachers have seen it as their job to teach learners how to apply theory, which they may well have learned in a very different context, either on the job, or in some practically contrived context which simulates aspects of the real world experience.

However, as this manual suggests, this may be to put the cart before the horse, since many, if not most, learners seem to benefit from being able to draw on their experience through opportunities for reflection and concept development, and to reapply to new experience what has become a much clearer understanding based on competence of which they can truly claim ownership. The suggestion is therefore that learners ought to be using practice in order to develop and test theory and not the other way round.

It is further suggested that most learners have a wealth of experience to draw on, which, however much lip-service is paid to it, tends to get sadly neglected even in the most carefully designed learning programmes. This is of course particularly true of adult learning programmes of all kinds, including staff development.

In the light of the current debate about the acquisition of competence in the workplace, this manual raises afresh some interesting questions about the merits of real versus simulated experience, and about the role of further education and training in the process of developing learners. It suggests a multitude of ways in which open-minded teachers can try out for themselves the merits of the experiential approach. It allows newcomers to the field to dip their big toes gently in the water, without feeling that a total conversion process is all that will achieve results. It allows teachers accustomed to a classroom and workshop context an opportunity to extend their practice little by little, so that they may begin to approach the perhaps new role of workplace tutor and assessor with confidence. It also offers some insight into the evaluation of such learning and testing processes, a topic likely to occupy educationists considerably in the next few years.

The manual is likely to be of particular interest to staff developers and tutors in further education and training.

FEU will be interested to receive feedback from any colleges which decide to trial-test the contents.

It remains to express our thanks to the Birmingham Polytechnic EDU team who developed the manual with the able support of Graham Gibbs, whose capacity for creative thinking contributed substantially to the finished result.

Elizabeth Simpson
Development Officer, FEU

1 Introduction

WHY USE THIS GUIDE ?

Most teachers and trainers seem to believe that you learn best by doing. But how is this rather general belief to be put into practice? In particular:

What ideas or theories are there to help us to explain and justify the belief that we learn best by doing?

Does everyone learn by doing in the same way or to the same extent?

What teaching and learning methods are there for us to use which involve learning by doing?

If our courses are re-designed to involve more learning by doing, what might they look like?

How is it possible to change our teaching to involve learning by doing when we are surrounded by constraints?

What can go wrong?

How can we encourage our colleagues to change their teaching to involve more learning by doing?

This guide addresses these questions in a direct way with straighforward explanations and concrete examples. Its emphasis is on practical teaching and learning methods for implementing learning by doing.

'Learning by doing', and the term 'experiential learning', are commonly used to refer to several different aspects of learning. This guide is not concerned with the assessment of 'prior learning': learning experiences which have taken place before learners enrol on courses and which are taken into account in the assessment of the course or the granting of exemptions from course components. Neither is this guide directly concerned with experiential learning in terms of personal development and the human potential and growth movements. Although aspects of personal development, such as the growth of autonomy, are important to learning by doing, it is a massive and separate topic and deserves its own separate guide.

HOW TO USE THE GUIDE

The guide is written to be used as a resource rather than as a book to be read right through. **Sections 4** and **5** are full of practical ideas for teaching methods and course designs and are meant to be dipped into. **Sections 2** and **3** provide the underlying ideas and **Section 6** provides follow-up information if you wish to apply the ideas.

Section 2 provides an explanation of experiential learning theory and the experiential learning cycle. It offers a way of structuring and sequencing learning to improve the effectiveness of learning from experience.

Section 3 describes the ways in which individuals differ in their preferred learning styles and in the way they handle their experiences. It explains some of the implications of experiential learning styles.

Section 4 describes a wide range of teaching and learning methods which implement each of the stages of experiential learning and which take learners round the experiential learning cycle.

Section 5 contains case studies of the use of experiential learning theory in course design and of the way experiential learning sessions are run. If you take experiential learning seriously, this is what your teaching may come to look like.

Section 6 contains exercises and materials to support staff development workshops designed to introduce teachers and trainers to experiential learning. It summarises the main assuptions underlying the adoption of experiential learning methods and lists the more common problems encountered in introducing experiential learning methods.

IS THIS GUIDE ENOUGH?

No it isn't! Inevitably the descriptions of teaching methods are brief and lack subtlety: sources are suggested for further reading. But reading on its own is not enough. **Section 6** offers workshops for introducing experiential learning methods to teaching staff experientially rather than through passive reading alone. But it is not until methods are tried out and teachers gain first hand experience of their use that their full value can be appreciated. To learn about experiential methods you have to use them and experience them, reflect on their use and experiment again. Ideally this should be done co-operatively so that teaching experiences can be discussed. Probably the ideal use of the guide would be on an in-service teacher training course where those on the course tried selected methods out in their teaching and then discussed what happened.

2 Experiential learning theory

It is common for courses to be described as either practical or theoretical: as either involving doing or involving thinking. Learning is seen to take place either 'on the job' or in the classroom. Even in courses which contain both elements they tend to be sharply divided. An academic teacher may present theory in a lecture in the classroom whilst a practical supervisor is in charge of the follow-up practical experience in a workshop.

It is also common for both types of course to have limited success.

It is not sufficient simply to have an experience in order to learn. Without reflecting upon this experience it may quickly be forgotten or its learning potential lost. It is from the feelings and thoughts emerging from this reflection that generalisations or concepts can be generated. And it is generalisations which enable new situations to be tackled effectively.

Similarly, if it is intended that behaviour should be changed by learning, it is not sufficient simply to learn new concepts and develop new generalisations. This learning must be tested out in new situations. The learner must make the link between theory and action by planing for that action, carrying it out, and then reflecting upon it, relating what happens back to the theory.

It is not enough just to do, and neither is it enough just to think. Nor is it enough simply to do and think. Learning from experience must involve links between the doing and the thinking. The four-stage model of learning by doing which is elaborated below is that of Kolb. Quite a few theorists have proposed cyclical models to explain how people learn from experience, but they all share the important features of Kolb's model which is itself derived from Lewin. Learning from experience involves **four** stages which follow each other in a cycle, as in the diagram on page 10.

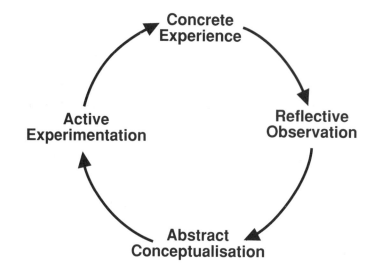

The terms used here as labels for the four stages come from Kolb's **Experiential Learning Theory**, and placed in this sequence they form the **experiential learning cycle.** The cycle can be entered by the learner at any point, but its stages must be followed in sequence.

EXAMPLE 1

A trainee nurse might start learning how to lift a patient by taking part in supervised practice with a dummy, which would give experience of (a simulation of) what it is like (stage **1** in the diagram below).

The Charge Nurse might then ask: "How did that feel? What might you have done differently?" to encourage the nurse to be reflective about the experience (stage **2**).

That night the nurse could look up, in a textbook, how to lift patients and read about the reasons for doing it in particular ways (stage **3**).

Next day, confronted with a real patient to lift, the nurse could think : "As a result of what happened yesterday, and because of what I read last night, I ought to do it like **this**" (stage **4**). This would provide a new experience and start the nurse on the next learning cycle.

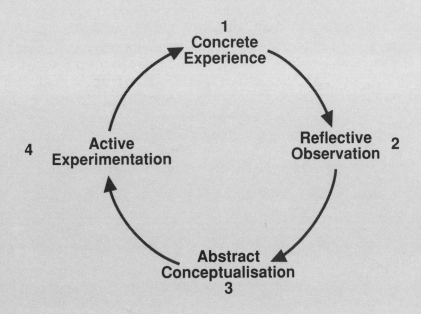

EXAMPLE 2

This learning cycle is exactly the same as that involved in carrying out experimental work. A chemistry course might involve the sequence of learning activities illustrated below:

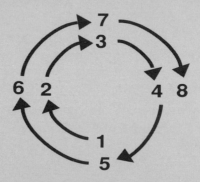

1 Taking notes in a lecture about a type of chemical reaction

2 Designing and running an experiment to test whether this type of reaction occurs with a particular group of elements

3 Gaining the experience of seeing what happens in the experiment

4 Looking at the results and comparing these with others' results

5 Discussing possible explanations of these results

6 Designing and running an experiment to test these alternative explanations

7 Gaining the experience of seeing what happens in this experiment

8 Looking at the results and comparing them with previous results

and so on, round and round the cycle, until an adequate understanding of the nature of the chemical reaction has been arrived at.

Exercise 1

Take a section of a course or a teaching or training session which you are responsible for and try to describe the sequence of learning activities involved in terms of the stages of the experiential learning cycle. Use the two examples above as models, and use this diagram and the space below it to plot the sequence.

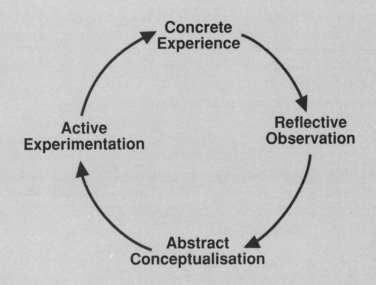

Stage 1:

Stage 2:

Stage 3:

Stage 4:

Stage 5:

Stage 6:

etc.

Which stages of the experiential learning cycle have been missed out (if any)? What could you add to complete the cycle(s)?

OVERVIEW

The following list of points may help to clarify what experiential learning is, and what it is not:

1   Learners are involved in an **active exploration of experience**. Experience is used to test out ideas and assumptions rather than to obtain practice passively. Practice can be very important but it is greatly enhanced by reflection.

2   Learners must selectively **reflect on their experience** in a critical way, rather than take experience for granted and assume that the experience on its own is sufficient.

3   The experience must matter to the learner. Learners must be **committed to the process of exploring and learning**.

4   There must be scope for the learner to exercise some **independence** from the teacher. Teachers have an important role in devising appropriate experiences and facilitating reflection. However the transmission of information is but a minor element and the teacher cannot experience what the learner experiences or reflect for the learner.

5   Experiential learning is **not the same as 'discovery' learning**. Learning by doing is not simply a matter of letting learners loose and hoping that they discover things for themselves in a haphazard way through sudden bursts of inspiration. The nature of the activity may be carefully designed by the teacher and the experience may need to be carefully reviewed and analysed afterwards for learning to take place. A crucial feature of experiential learning is the **structure** devised by the teacher within which learning takes place.

6   **Openness to experience** is necessary for learners to have the evidence upon which to reflect. It is therefore crucial to establish an appropriate emotional tone for learners: one which is safe and supportive, and which encourages learners to **value their own experience** and to trust themselves to draw conclusions from it. This openness may not exist at the outset but may be fostered through successive experiences of the experiential learning cycle.

7   Experiential learning involves a **cyclical sequence of learning activities**. Teaching methods can be selected to provide a structure to each stage of the cycle, and to take learners through the appropriate sequence.

    Sections 4 and **5** provide practical advice on appropriate teaching methods.

Further reading

Boud, D., Keogh, R.   **Reflection: Turning Experience Into Learning**
and Walker, D. (Eds.) Kogan Page, London. 1985.

Kolb, D. A.   **Experiential Learning - Experience as the Source of Learning and Development** Prentice-Hall, New Jersey. 1984.

3 Learning styles

Just as courses may be seen to be either mainly practical or mainly theoretical, so individuals may have particular preferences in their learning. While one person might prefer to formulate plans and define potential problems, another might prefer to get on and carry out the plans. There are distinct learning styles associated with each of the stages of the experiential learning cycle.

These differences in style were illustrated graphically in a computing course. At the start of this computing course the students were set an open-ended computing problem to work on alone over the next four weeks. They then met to compare solutions to the problem, but also to compare the different ways in which they went about working on the problem. Three of the students displayed dramatically different styles:

Student A went straight to a computer keyboard and started keying in segments of a program. She didn't analyse the nature of the problem. As soon as it became apparent that the programming routines being written didn't work, new routines were written out and immediately tested in a trial and error way: mostly error. This student had created dozens of programming routines, none of which got close to solving the problem. She seemed not to learn from her mistakes.

Student B appeared to start off like student A, going straight to the keyboard. He selected a procedure which he knew and implemented it. He wrote an extensive, detailed and complete programme which ran successfully, but which solved a problem quite different from the one which was set. He was unaware that he had tackled the wrong problem because he was so busy getting on with the task.

Student C became intrigued by the problem itself and its underlying features. She started reading about this kind of problem and the reading led her into related areas which also contained intriguing problems. She could talk animatedly about the topic in general in an abstract way but hadn't even started writing any programming code to produce a solution.

In terms of the experiential learning cycle, these students were stuck at one part of the cycle to the virtual exclusion of the other three.

Exercise 2

See if you can place the three students on the cycle in the diagram below by identifying which aspects of the experiential learning cycle each exhibits and misses out.

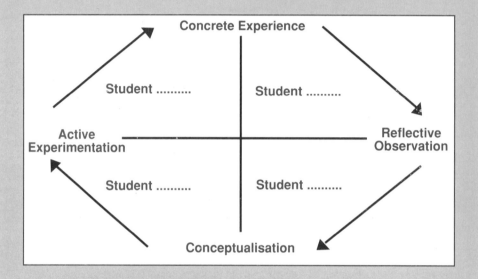

Locate students A, B and C on this diagram, and explain your reasons for each:

Student A

Student B

Student C

We have located these three students in the diagram below. We have done so by thinking about why each of these students failed to solve the problem.

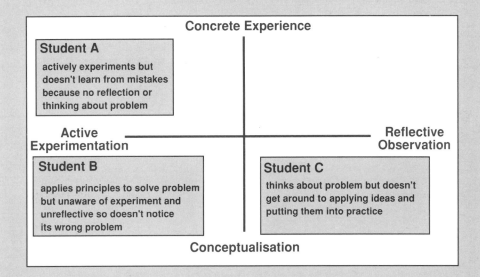

Student A failed because she experimented without learning from her mistakes. She didn't start from an analysis of the problem (conceptualisation) and didn't seem to reflect on the outcomes of her experiments (reflection). All she did was try things out (active experimentation) and change tack when she experienced things not working out (experience). She might be quite good at practical work and experimentation, but she won't learn from this.

Student B failed because he didn't even notice that his solution was solving the wrong problem: he was not aware of his own experience. This style characteristically involves 'premature closure' or rushing to a single solution without generating or considering alternatives. He might be very good at working through procedures which apply theory to a specific situation, but this won't neccessarily help him.

Student C might be quite creative and admirably thoughtful about what she is doing, but until she gets down and tries her ideas out in practice she isn't going to get anywhere. At some point she has to narrow down the scope of the possibilities in front of her and get her hands on the keyboard and see what happens when she tries things out.

In order to learn effectively from experience it is necessary to utilise the abilities associated with each of the four learning styles in turn. These abilities are illustrated in the diagram below:

Experience	
Can carry our plans	**Imaginative, good at generating ideas**
Interested in action and results	**Can view situation from different angles**
Adapts to immediate circumstances	**Open to experience**
Trial and error style	**Recognises problems**
Sets objectives	**Investigates**
Sets schedules	**Senses opportunities**
Experimentation	**Reflection**
Good at practical applications	**Ability to create theoretical models**
Makes decisions	**Compares alternatives**
Focusses efforts	**Defines problems**
Does well when there is one answer	**Establishes criteria**
Evaluates plans	**Formulates hypotheses**
Selects from alternatives	
Conceptualisation	

Abilities associated with each stage of the learning cycle

Rather than have extreme styles, therefore, it is preferable to be adaptable and to operate in the style appropriate to each successive stage of the experiential learning cycle at different stages in a learning task. It can be valuable for students to recognise their own habitual learning style and to recognise the characteristics of learning tasks as this may help them to become more flexible in meeting the varied demands of learning situations.

The students of computing were encouraged to discuss their learning styles and were then put in project groups which mixed styles so that students experienced the ways in which others worked. Each week the teaching session was started with a discussion of how the project groups had gone about tackling their tasks in order to raise students' awareness of the alternative approaches possible.

Several questionnaires and checklists are available to enable the quick diagnosis of learning styles. There are numerous other frameworks for making sense of differences in learning style but the framework outlined here is the most useful one in relation to learning by doing.

Further reading

For a short experiential learning styles inventory and explanation of learning styles:

Kolb, D.A., Rubin, I.M. and McIntyre, J.M.	**Organisational Psychology: An Experiential Approach** Prentice Hall. 1974.

For a more extensive questionnaire and analysis of learning styles:

Honey, P. and Mumford, A.	**The Manual of Learning Styles** Peter Honey, Maidenhead. 1986.

For a learners' guide to learning styles and how to change your learning style:

Honey, P. and Mumford, A.	**Using Your Learning Styles** Peter Honey, Maidenhead. 1986.

4 Practical methods to implement the experiential learning cycle

The practical teaching and learning methods described in this section are categorised according to the phase of the experiential learning cycle with which they are primarily concerned, as illustrated in the diagrams below:

4.1 Planning for experience

This section is concerned with methods for preparing learners prior to experiences so that they make the most of those experiences: for example through action planning and the negotiation of learning contracts.

4.2 Increasing awareness of experience

This section is concerned with methods for heightening learners' awareness of their experiences so that they notice more and have more material upon which to reflect afterwards: for example through the use of log books.

4.3 Reviewing and reflecting upon experience

This section is concerned with what happens after learning experiences and how learning points can be drawn out through structured reflection: for example through the use of video recordings and self-assessment.

4.4 Providing substitute experiences

This section is concerned with ways of providing classroom-based experiences as substitutes for work or other experience: for example through the use of role plays.

4.1   Planning for experience

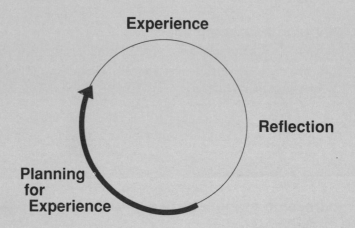

4.1.1 Action plans

4.1.2 Setting objectives

4.1.3 Designing experiments

4.1.4 Observation checklists

4.1.5 Devising criteria

4.1.6 Learning contracts

4.1.7 Action research

4.1.1   Action plans

An action plan is simply a written list of things to do. A trainee painter could draw up an action plan for the sequence of tasks and decisions which need to be made in decorating a room. This could be done by :

(a) reviewing notes from a classroom session concerned with general rules concerning how to undertake decorations (e.g. the order in which wallpaper should be hung) and

(b) applying these general principles to the job in hand.

Such a list could be kept at hand in order to keep a check on the experience of undertaking the decoration task.

4.1.2   Setting objectives

Although it is common for teachers to set objectives for learners, learners can also set objectives for themselves. Before embarking upon an experience of some kind, learners can sit down and write out: "After this experience I will be able to ...." and specify what will have been learnt. This can be an excellent way of focussing attention on important aspects the experience by providing a reminder of what function the experience is supposed to have. Such a set of objectives (it may only need to be a few to be useful) can also provide a valuable aid to reflection and self-assessment after the experience.

4.1.3   Designing experiments

In many practically based scientific and technical subjects, learners undertake experimental work in the laboratory or workshop. It is common for the teacher to design the experiments for the learners to execute, sometimes giving learners little to do except follow instructions. For learners to be more involved in experimental work and more alive to their experience of it, it is important for them to be involved in at least some aspects of the experimental design. It may be possible simply to pose a problem, ask "How are you going to be able to measure X or find a value for Y ?" and leave the learners to design their own experiments. It may be that you have to provide most of the experimental design, but can leave some details unresolved, to be discussed and agreed before work begins. It may be that for practical reasons you have to have prepared equipment and facilities in advance and there is little scope for variation. Nevertheless there is still scope for students to speculate about possible experimental designs beforehand so that the actual experimental design is seen as one of a range of possibilities instead of simply taken for granted as **the** design. As outlined in **Section 2**, scientific method is fundamentally the same as the experiential learning cycle, and learners should not miss out stages merely for the sake of convenience or saving time.

4.1.4   Observation checklists

Much experience is gained through seeing how others do things, or what goes on in situations. However, if you are new to a situation, you may not know what to look for and it can be very easy to lose attention and to notice very little. This problem can be eased with the use of a simple observation checklist which lists things to look out for and perhaps asks for the recording of events and how often they happened.

Ready-made observation checklists of some sophistication are available for example for observing school teachers in action. Simple checklists can be devised by the learners themselves. For example, prior to a small group of trainee nurses seeing a Staff Nurse administering medication on a ward, there could be a short discussion of what to look out for, and a brief checklist drawn up. After the round, this could be used to structure a short discussion which encourages reflection on what had been seen, and what significance these observations had.

The example of an observation sheet on page 27 is for use in observing and giving feedback on group leaders or committee chairpersons. The sheet identifies categories of leadership behaviour, gives examples or definitions of each, and has space for recording the number of occasions on which each type of behaviour was observed and for comments. The use of this observation checklist would be likely to lead to much more being noticed and so more being able to be reported back to the person being observed. What is reported back could also be backed up by evidence rather than being purely subjective.

OBSERVER CHECKLIST

Observer ....   Subject ....

Category	Definition	Number	Comments
PROPOSING			
Initiating	putting forward ideas, suggesting action, telling others what to do		
Developing	adding to suggestions put forward by others		
REACTING			
Supporting	supporting someone else; agreeing with their ideas and opinions		
Disagreeing	disagreeing with someone else's ideas or opinions		
CLARIFYING			
Seeking information	seeking to know the ideas or opinions of others		
Testing understanding	checking you have understood what someone has said		
Summarising	briefly restating what has already been said		
Giving information	putting forward opinions or information		
CONTROLLING			
Interrupting	talking across another person		
Bringing in	inviting another person to speak		

4.1.5   Devising criteria

It can be difficult to undertake a task well if you don't have much idea what would count as doing it well. If you didn't know what a good weld should look like, for example, it would be unlikely that you would notice what you were doing wrong while you were undertaking the weld: your experience would be largely wasted. It can often make an enormous difference to how attentive and careful and 'self-concious' a learner is when undertaking a practical task if the learner has a clear idea of the criteria which will be used to judge the outcome of the work. A discussion of the criteria to be used in marking a project report will focus learners' attention on important aspects of the project work. An example of devising criteria and using them for subsequent self-assessment can be found in **Section 5.1.**

4.1.6   Learning contracts

Learning contracts combine several elements of planning descibed above, especially setting objectives, devising criteria and formulating action plans. A learning contract is an agreement to undertake some action leading to learning. The agreement could be with a trainer, teacher or a group of fellow learners. A trainee learning about word processing could devise a contract which read:

> "I contract to use the MAILMERGE facility to address letters to members of my child's school's PTA. between now and the next session, and to report to the group on how difficult I found it."

The learner would normally report back on the completion of learning contracts. The completion of such a contract, agreed with the teacher, can be used in assessment. An example of this can be found in **Section 5.4.**

In some educational settings the entire curriculum, including assessment, is based on learning contracts. A more formal and detailed process is then neccessary. Structured approaches to learning contracts, such as the one listed below, can also be valuable in making informal learning more rigorous where there is no external check on learning outcomes. The process described here is based on the work of Malcolm Knowles and has eight stages:

1 Diagnose your learning needs

The gap between where you are now and where you want to get to identifies your learning needs. This may involve analysing the skills and knowledge required to perform a particular job (for example what is involved in organising yourself more efficiently) and identifying where you stand at the moment in relation to these skills. You might decide that the organisational skills involved include:
– filing
– work scheduling and deadline setting
– diary keeping
– establishing procedures for routine work
– reviewing your work periodically and adjusting priorities

You might also decide that you already know how to keep an adequate diary, and that you really need to focus on filing, routine procedures and work scheduling.

2 Specify your learning objectives

Learning objectives are what you hope to learn by doing things and/or what you will be able to do once you have learnt. For example, you might want to learn how to become more efficient in your work *so that you can accomplish 20% more work in a day.* You would probably need to divide your objectives up so that they are sufficiently specific to guide your learning.

3 Specify learning resources and strategies

This involves identifying where you will find out what you need to know, and who can help you, as well as how you intend to use these resources. Strategies might also involve a timetable or intermediate goals and deadlines, identifying steps on the way to achieving your learning goals and the sequence of learning activities involved in achieving them.

4 Specify evidence of accomplishment

How will you (or anyone else?) know that you have achieved your objectives? What would you be able to do, or have to show, which would demonstrate your achievements? What this evidence looks like then becomes the specific focus of your learning.

5 Specify how the evidence will be validated

What criteria are appropriate for judging your learning outcomes? Who should make these judgements and how? In a formal situation this might be a tutor or trainer. In an informal situation this might involve self-assessment.

6 Review your contract

At this point you would be ready to show your proposed learning contract to someone else to review it. In a formal context this might be in order to decide whether the contract, if fulfilled, would meet some specified criteria for a qualification. A teacher, in reviewing such a contract, might suggest that the contract is over-ambitious or requires a clearer specification of what the outcome should look like. In an informal situation a review might involve a friend reading through it and asking for clarification on points which seem ambiguous or unclear.

7 Carry out the contract

It is often the case that once work to fulfil a learning contract has begun, the goals need to be re-cast and alternative learning strategies adopted. There should be an opportunity to re-negotiate aspects of the contract to take account of early experiences of trying to fulfil it. In the example in **Section 5.4** there is an opportunity for trainee lecturers and their tutor to modify project agreement forms in the light of experience, provided both parties agree to the changes.

8 Evaluate your learning

The specification of the contract, and especially the specification of what evidence of accomplishment should look like and how it should be judged, makes evaluation of learning relatively straightforward. It is crucial that, after the negotiation and completion of a learning contract, new criteria or tests are not introduced. A properly formulated contract embodies the means for its assessment. If the learner is going to go on and devise further learning contracts then this is the time to reflect on the whole process in order to learn how to devise appropriate contracts and means of validating their accomplishment.

Further reading

Knowles, M. S.   **Self-directed Learning: A Guide for Learners and Teachers** Associated Press, New York. 1975.

4.1.7 Action research

Action research is simply the application of the experiential learning cycle to research activities designed to improve practice. It involves four stages:

1   develop a plan of action to improve what is already happening

2   act to carry out the plan

3   observe the effects of the action

4   reflect on these effects as a basis for future planning and action.

This would lead to further planning and action in a continuing cycle of experimentation and improvement. The starting-point of such a cycle of action research might itself be an observation of a problem in your own work. For example, a nurse might notice that some people on a ward are at a loose end while others are rushing around. Some reflection on this problem might lead to the analysis that responsibilities have not been divided up appropriately. An action plan might involve changing some individuals' responsibilities (with due regard to union agreements, relationships and teamwork issues). The ward could then operate for a week with this new division of responsibilities, during which time the effect on workloads and delays in getting jobs done could be monitored. At the end of the week those involved could report on what had actually happened and how they had found the week. This might lead to a new understanding as to how to share the work, new work practices and new experiences.

Action research was developed as a way for teachers to improve their effectiveness in their own classrooms but it can be used in any context where people want to learn how to improve their work.

Further reading

Kemmis, S. and
McTaggart, R.   **The Action Research Planner** Deakin
                       University, Victoria. 1982.

4.2   Increasing awareness of experience

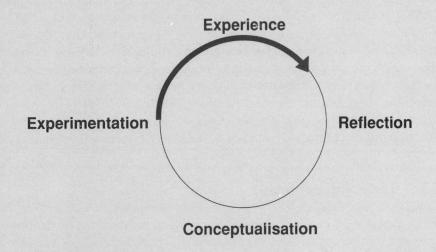

4.2.1 Log books

4.2.2 Listening exercises

4.2.3 Questions

4.2.4 Increasing awareness of feelings

4.2.5 Silent demonstrations

4.2.1 Log books

Log books are used quite commonly in laboratory work; they are for recording what is going on in experiments, as it happens, for subsequent analysis and interpretation. Log books are also sometimes used in art and design and architecture courses where it is important that fleeting emotional responses to draft ideas and plans, rough sketches and the like are not lost, but are collected to help subsequent development of the ideas. Such jottings are especially useful in discussions with teachers and to aid reflection. Log books are distinct from portfolios, which are more collections of work in progress, and from diaries, which are more for the subsequent reflection and analysis of experience. At its best, the process of keeping a log heightens and focusses experience.

4.2.2 Listening exercises

Many experiences involve listening: listening to instructions or demonstrations, or listening to others in a certain situation, for example a trainee teacher listening to the way an experienced teacher handles questions from a class. There are simple exercises which can be run to improve learners' attentiveness and ability to respond to and recall what others say.

In the example of a listening exercise on page 35 the focus is on active listening: listening in a way which helps the speaker. Listening in this way requires great attentiveness as well as other skills. This example is intended to illustrate the way such an exercise can run and the type of handout which can be used. The model of listening embodied in this material is not meant to be prescriptive.

Listening exercise

Stage 1   **Working alone**

3 minutes   Students should think back to a situation when they were trying to tell someone something, or to talk through a problem, and the other person was not listening or was doing other things which annoyed them or got in the way of what they were trying to say. The students should try writing down what the things were which the listener was doing which they'd rather they hadn't done.

Stage 2   **In pairs**

12 minutes   Students should tell their 'story' to their group of four. One of the four should make notes of all the things people do when they are not listening properly or effectively.

Stage 3   **Whole group plenary**

15 minutes   The tutor should list points on the board, from each group in turn, about what listeners do wrong in listening, then hand out the list below of characteristics of effective and ineffective listening and discuss in the light of points groups have already raised.

30 minutes   *Stages 1 - 3 ensure that participants start from their own experience, but they can be omitted and a briefer exercise started from stage 4.*

Stage 4   **In groups of three**

5 minutes   The tutor should instruct one of the three to tell one of the others about a difficulty or problem in their life at the moment (e.g. whether to move house, which course to take next, whether to change their car, problems with their parents or whatever). The third student should use the handout as an observation checklist and watch how the listener listens and make notes under each of the headings. The groups of three should be stopped after five minutes.

Stage 5   **In groups of three**

5 minutes   The observer should tell the listener what he or she saw and noted down. Then the person talking should tell the listener how he or she found the listener. Finally the listener should have a chance to report on how easy or difficult the listening was, referring to the categories on the checklist.

Stages 4 and 5 should be repeated so that all three in each group gain experience of active listening (30 minutes in all)

Stage 6   **Whole group plenary**

30 minutes   The whole class should discuss the experience of listening, and being listened to, in an active way in the groups. The session should finish off with a 'round' in which each person in turn says which of the listening techniques was most effective and worth using in future.

60 minutes   (or 90 minutes including stages 1 - 3)

Ineffective Listening	Effective Listening

Non-verbal behaviour

Listener looks bored, uninterested or judgemental; avoids eye contact; displays distracting manerisms (doodles, plays with a paper clip, etc.)	Listener maintains positive posture; avoids distracting mannerisms; keeps attention focussed on speaker; maintains eye contact; nods and smiles when appropriate

Focus of attention

Listener shifts focus of attention to himself/herself "When something like that happens to me, I...."	Listener keeps focus of comments on the speaker: "When that happened, what did you do?"

Acceptance

Listener fails to accept speaker's ideas and feelings: "I think it would have been better to...."	Listener accepts ideas and feelings "That's an interesting idea; can you say more about it?"

Empathy

Listener fails to empathise: "I don't see why you felt that"	Listener empathises "So when that happened, you felt angry."

Probing

Listener fails to probe into an area, to follow up on an idea or feeling.	Listener probes in a helpful way; "Could you tell me more about what led you to feel that way?" and follows up: "You said that..."

Paraphrasing

Listener fails to check by restating in own words important statements made by the speaker	Listener paraphrases at an appropriate time to check understanding

Summarising

Listener fails to summarise	Listener summarises progress of the conversation from time to time.

Advising

Listener narrows the range of suggesting a 'correct' course of action	Listener widens the range of ideas ideas by by suggesting a number of alternatives

4.2.3 Questions

Some aspects of experiences are puzzling (e.g."Why ever did they do **that**?") and it is often not possible to get immediate solutions to these puzzles. Puzzles and questions which arise can distract learners from their immediate experience. However, they can be invaluable afterwards to help reflection and to link the experience to concepts and generalisations. It can be helpful to have a note pad to hand and quickly write down the questions that arise so that they are cleared out of the way and do not interfere with attention. Also, if only questions are allowed to be written down, attention can be directed to puzzling, anomalous or incomprehensible aspects of the experience, should this be useful, and these questions used as a basis for reflection on these aspects afterwards.

4.2.4   Increasing awareness of feelings: ground rules for groups

Groups often behave in ways which have the effect of avoiding the expression of strong feelings or denying that they exist. Some simple 'ground rules' can dramatically affect the ways groups operate so that individuals' feelings are expressed and become a legitimate focus for the group's attention. Individuals become more aware of their own feelings and learn to respond to these feelings and deal with them more appropriately. They also become more aware of others' feelings.

Ground rules for groups:

1   Make "I" statements instead of neutral or general statements. Instead of "We ought to move on" say: "I'd like to move on".

2   Own feelings. Instead of just being angry and covering this up, own the feeling and say: "I feel angry".

3   Avoid blaming others for your feelings. Instead of saying: "You make me angry, doing that" say: "When you do that I feel angry".

4   Don't speak for others, especially not for their feelings. Instead of saying: "We are all bored with this" say: "I feel bored with this. How do you feel?"

5   Avoid judgements of situations or of others. Instead of saying: "This is boring" say: "I feel bored with this". Instead of saying: "You are wrong" say: "I disagree with you".

4.2.5 Silent demonstrations

It is sometimes important for learners to observe an expert performing a task before gaining experience of performing the task themselves. But getting learners to really pay attention during a demonstration can often be a problem. Paradoxically, the usual 'voice-over' commentary during demonstrations, which is intended to direct learners' attention towards key actions or features of the demonstration, can have the opposite effect. Hearing a full description of what is going on, learners don't bother to observe carefully. (On aircraft do you watch the demonstration of how to use a life jacket when you can hear the recorded commentary over the public adress system?)

You may have noticed, whilst listening to the radio, the phenomenon of increased attention being achieved through reducing the amount of information available. For example, radio plays or wildlife documentaries can hold the attention and increase an active awareness of the experience in a way which television often fails to do. Television wildlife documentaries with voice-overs added as an afterthought, in particular, seem to shift the mind into neutral.

One way to heighten attention and make observation more acute, therefore, is to make it more demanding. An effective way to do this is to use a silent demonstration and follow it with reflection on what was observed. For example, medical students could be told:

> "I am going to suture this wound. I want you to watch carefully. When I have finished I am going to ask you for a full description of what I did. While you are watching and making mental notes, I'd also like you to think about why I used the materials and instruments I did and why I used them in the way I did. I shan't say anything or point out what I am doing, so you will have to watch carefully."

This clinical teacher is also using questions (see **Section 4.2.3**) and could have added an observation checklist (see **Section 4.1.4**). If what is being observed is potentially complex and confusing, the task of watching a silent demonstration can be divided between learners: for example one medical student could have been asked to note the sequence of actions, another the instruments used, and so on.

4.3   Reviewing and reflecting upon experience

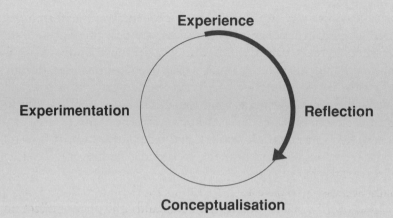

This section is concerned with methods which help learners to reflect on experiences they have had: to obtain full accounts of what took place, to make value judgements about those events, to categorise experience and to move on to analyse the experience and draw out learning points for the future. The foundation for effective reflection is laid through awareness of experience, which is dealt with in **Section 4.2**. Most of the techniques described here could be used effectively in conjunction with the techniques for providing substitute experiences described in **Section 4.4**.

4.3.1 Diaries

4.3.2 Using video and audio recordings

4.3.3 Peer appraisal

4.3.4 Structured discussions

4.3.5 Structured de-briefing

4.3.6 Self-assessment

4.3.7 Reflection checklists and questionnaires

4.3.8 'Shared time' and 'mutual interviewing'

4.3.9 Modelling reflection

4.3.1 Diaries

Diaries are different from logs (see **Section 4.2.1**) in that they are written after the experience rather than during it. During a work placement, for example, a diary might be written each evening, after a day's work. Diaries can often be most effective in the form: "Dear Diary, ..." since letter writing can be easier than 'report writing' and also encourages a personal and emotional response to experiences. Diaries can be used simply to record immediate experiences and reactions to these, or they can go one step further and start to analyse these experiences and draw conclusions from them. It can sometimes be helpful to have two columns on a page: one to record the events and the other for feelings and reactions to these. It is usually neccessary to have a strict routine for filling in a diary in order to keep up regular entries: much of the detail and feeling of recollection fades within 24 hours.

Further reading

Holly, M.L.   **Keeping A Personal-Professional Journal**
                       DeakinUniversity, Victoria. 1984.

4.3.2 Using video and audio recordings

Video recordings can provide a powerful tool to aid reflection on experience. Some areas use video a great deal in this way: for example in 'micro-teaching' to train specific teaching skills, and in social worker and counsellor training in interviewing and interpersonal skills training. Used with appropriate questions, as with 'Interpersonal Process Recall' (IPR), video can be used to cue very detailed recall of exactly what was going on in your mind at the time, and in particular what feelings were being experienced. It is often best to leave control of the recording in the hands of the trainees, encouraging them to stop the video playback to discuss points when they recognise something of significance to them in their experience of the situation which was recorded.

Questions which are useful to help reflection during video replays include:

What was going on then?

How did you feel at that point?

Have you felt like that before?

What were you thinking?

How were the others feeling and what were they thinking?

What else could you have done at that point?

What stopped you?

If you had done that, how would it have felt?

Have you felt like that before? Tell me about that time.

What would you have liked to say to the others at that point?

What would they have liked you to have done?

What did you want to happen?

What do you think the others wanted to happen?

What did you want the others to say?

Was there any risk for you?

Were there any risks for the others?

Would you like to start the tape again?

When video recording equipment is not available, a simple audio cassette recorder can provide an acceptable alternative in situations where what is said is more important than what is done.

Further reading

Zuber-Skerritt, O.   **Video in Higher Education** Kogan Page, London. 1984.

4.3.3 Peer appraisal

It can be very useful to get feedback from someone who watched you while you were undertaking a task. However people find it rather difficult to say: "You did this well and this badly" and even more difficult to listen to and accept this kind of personal feedback. There is often a tendency to dwell on critical points and to be defensive. The sequence outlined on page 44 is designed to make the process of peer appraisal easier, more positive and more forward looking.

There are several features of this process which are worth highlighting:

– There is an emphasis on having evidence of what went on. If either the trainee or the appraiser were to say that something happened, it would be important to ask: "How do you know?".

– It takes into account that those involved have feelings about what went on and provides opportunities at the beginning and end to express these.

– The trainee gets a chance to appraise himself/herself first, before the appraiser. This encourages reflection. It is common for the trainee to notice many of the points the trainer would want to comment on.

– The positive points are dealt with before the negative points, and the negative points are followed by some planning about what might be done instead next time.

Further reading

Gibbs, G. and   **53 Interesting Ways to Appraise Your**
Colling, C.   **Teaching** Technical and Educational Services, Bristol. 1987.

Trainee	Both	Appraiser
	1 Prior work Observation Notes Reflections Documents	
	2 Feelings?	

DESCRIPTION

Trainee	Both	Appraiser
3 What you noticed/observed about yourself and about others		4 What you noticed/ observed about the trainee

POSITIVE EVALUATION

Trainee	Both	Appraiser
5 List things you did well and how you know		6 List other things you think the trainee did well

NEGATIVE EVALUATION

Trainee	Both	Appraiser
7 List things that didn't go so well, and how you know		8 List other things you think the trainee didn't do so well and how you know

9 Convert each item into a problem question:

e.g. "How might you do .... next time" ?

ACTION PLANNING

Trainee	Both	Appraiser
10 In the light of the above, what you propose to do differently or learn about		11 What you would like the trainee to do differently or learn about, and how you can help
12 What you think the appraiser or others can do to help		13 Feedback to the appraiser
	14 Feelings?	

4.3.4 Structured discussions

Groups of learners can benefit from sharing their experiences. However, an unstructured discussion can often turn into a rambling sequence of anecdotes. It can be useful to structure discussion so as to move the learners from identifying key incidents in their experience, through analysis of these experiences, to drawing general conclusions from the collection of experiences discussed. For example a group of trainee social workers could reflect on their experience of dealing with difficult clients. The discussion could take this form:

Stage 1   On your own, think back to two occasions on which you dealt with a difficult client: one which you handled rather well, and one which you feel you handled badly. Make some notes about these situations: what went on, what the outcome was, and so on.

Stage 2   In pairs, describe these two situations to each other. Try to understand what it was about your partner's handling of the situations which was good or bad.

Stage 3   In groups of four, start listing characteristics of handling difficult clients well and handling them badly. Someone take notes in the form: "When we handle difficult clients well we: ....".

Stage 4   In the whole group, go round each group of four in turn picking up one 'good' point and one 'bad' point. List these on the board for all to see. When all the points have been collected and displayed, move into an open discussion of general features of handling difficult clients well.

This discussion structure is known as snowballing, or pyramidding, and is a simple and easy way to pool the experiences of a group in a productive way.

Further reading

Habeshaw, S., Habeshaw, T. and Gibbs, G.   **53 Interesting Things To Do In Your Seminars** Technical and Educational Services, Bristol. 1984.

4.3.5 Structured de-briefing

Common problems with discussions, or 'de-briefings', after an experience (or after substitute experience such as a role play) include:

- they often lurch from superficial descriptions of what happened to premature conclusions about what to do next, without adequate reflection or analysis;

- if the experience has been especially powerful then discussion may never get further than description of what happened or of the feelings associated with the experience;

- if description and feelings are not dealt with adequately, learners may return to these at a later stage when they should be considering implications and action plans.

The diagram on page 47 relates the stages of a full structured de-briefing to the stages of the experiential learning cycle:

Description: What happened? Don't make judgements yet or try to draw conclusions; simply describe.

Feelings: What were your reactions and feelings? Again don't move on to analysing these yet.

Evaluation: What was good and bad about the experience? Make value judgements.

Analysis: What sense can you make of the situation? Bring in ideas from outside the experience to help you. What was really going on? Were different people's experiences similar or different in important ways?

Conclusions: What can be concluded, in a general sense, from
(general)   these experiences and the analyses you have undertaken?

Conclusions: What can be concluded about your own specific,
(specific)   unique, personal situation or way of working?

Conclusions: What can be concluded about your own specific,
(specific)   unique, personal situation or way of working?

Personal action What are you going to do differently in this type of
plans: situation next time? What steps are you going to take
                      on the basis of what you have learnt?

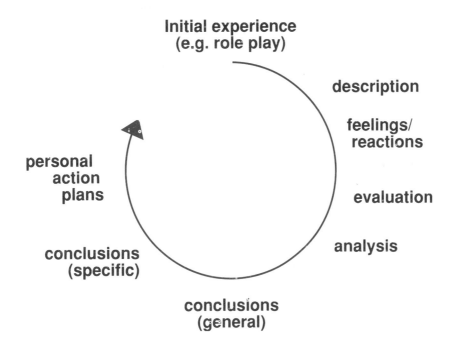

De-briefing sequence following the experiential learning cycle

If you have enough time you should try to move logically from one step to the next. Learners often have trouble moving cleanly from one stage to the next and so it can be useful to change the process at each stage as well as the focus of attention, so as to mark the transitions positively. For example, noting descriptions could be undertaken individually, reporting feelings could be handled in pairs, discussion of analysis could be undertaken in fours, general conclusions drawn in a whole group, specific conclusions worked through alone and displayed on posters and personal action plans identified individually before reporting them to the whole group in a final 'round'. It may be important for a group leader to be very explicit about which stage of the process the group should be working on, for example:

> "We've now spent some time on the feelings involved in those experiences. Let's leave those behind and move on to evaluating those experiences. What was good and what was bad about them. Try not to fall back into describing your feelings again, but move on to evaluating the experience."

4.3.6   Self-assessment

While comments and appraisal from the trainer or peers may be valuable, ultimately it is the individual's self-assessment which matters. Evidence from a video recording or observations by others are only inputs into self-assessment. Both the start and the conclusion of the process of reflection should be self-assessment: initially of direct experience, and finally of what personal conclusions can be drawn, having analysed that experience. This self-assessment should ideally lead into planning for the next experience, in the form: "Next time I will...." (see **Section 4.2**).

It can make it much more likely that this self-assessment goes on, is valued, and becomes a normal part of the learning process, if it is taken seriously in the formal assessment system. For example, in a Geography Department students are required to submit self-assessment sheets, listing strong and weak features of their work and a self-assigned grade, with every piece of work submitted for assessment, from fieldwork reports to essays.

Further reading

Boud, D.	**Studies in Self-Assessment** HERDSA Green Guide No. 5. 1986. Available from SCED, EDU, Birmingham Polytechnic.

4.3.7   Reflection checklists and questionnaires

Learners can often have difficulty getting started on reflecting about their experience. It can be useful to have checklists or questionnaires to get them going. For example, a Health Visitors course uses a checklist containing a list of all the skills which are involved in different aspects of the work. When the trainees have tutorial discussions with an experienced Health Visitor, they go through this list as a way of recalling incidents which involved using these skills. The list is also used for assessment purposes.

A questionnaire can be used to elicit attitudes and emotional responses by listing statements such as: "When I visit senile patients I find it difficult to treat them as people" to which the trainees respond by indicating the extent to which the statement is true for them. It is easy to generate such lists. It can be useful to leave spaces at the end for the learners to add statements of their own about how they feel about aspects of their experience.

The checklist on page 50 was developed to help students to reflect about how they revise for exams. After working through such a checklist a student would be likely to have recalled experiences in vivid detail and have plenty to contribute to a discussion, leading to plans about how to be successful in exams in the future.

REVISION CHECKLIST

Here is a list of things which students do which results in their doing badly during exams. Tick those you have done yourself in the past and add any others you think you have done.

1 Arrive late and flustered

2 Don't read the instructions properly and answer the wrong number of questions.

3 Write illegibly.

4 Don't read the questions properly, and answer questions which haven't been asked, or fail to answer the questions which have been asked.

5 Don't check answers for silly mistakes.

6 Budget time badly so that most of the time is spent on a few questions, leaving little or no time for others.

7 Spend a long time on questions which carry few marks and little time on the questions which carry most marks.

8 Spend lots of time trying to improve on already complete and good answers (where few if any extra marks are possible) instead of spending time on poor and incomplete answers (where additional marks could be picked up easily).

9 Write furiously, in the belief that quantity gains marks rather than quality.

10 Leave before the end.

11 Panic.

Add your own

12 ....

13 ....

4.3.8 'Shared time' and 'mutual interviewing'

The unwritten rules of everyday conversation frequently act to limit the depth and value of reflection: silences are quickly filled, difficult and emotionally powerful topics are quickly skated over, listeners interrupt and tell you about their experiences which are irrelevant to you, and the vociferous grab most of the available time. In large groups these problems are magnified: the topic of conversation changes rapidly, is seldom directly related to individual concerns and tends to drift inconclusively while those involved seem unaware of the passage of time.

What an individual needs to make the most of reflection is a guaranteed amount of time spent exclusively on matters of personal concern and an audience who will help rather than hinder. The simplest way to achieve this is through 'shared time':

- learners form pairs (or threes)

- the total time available is divided equally between the pair (or three)

- in turns, each learner has a given time allocation for reflection: no more and no less

- the listeners only listen, they do not speak

- even if the learner whose turn it is remains silent, the listeners do not interrupt. Silent reflection can be very powerful!

As little as one minute each can be more productive than a twenty minute chat.

The listener can play a fuller role by posing questions which encourage the speaker to pursue reflections in more depth, to address difficult issues and to get 'unstuck' when reflection is proving unproductive. In 'mutual interviewing' the same ground rules apply as in 'shared time', but the listener may also ask non-directive questions of the following kind:

Description

"Can you describe it in more detail? What exactly happened?"

"What did you do?"

"What were you thinking/feeling at that point?"

Judgement

"What was good/bad about that?"

"Is that situation easy/difficult for you?"

Analysis

"In what way is that like experiences you have had before?"

"Why do you think that happened?"

Conclusions

"What else could you have done?"

"Faced with that situation again, what would you do?"

It is crucial that the 'interviewers' don't start answering their own questions or giving advice or the reflection will collapse into a conversation. A discussion of the interesting ideas and issues which emerge can take place after each learner has had a chance to reflect.

4.3.9 Modelling reflection

When you ask learners to sit down together and discuss what they have just experienced, they often find this difficult. They may be unsure what it is about their experience they ought to be talking about or what is permissible and what is not (especially if the focus is on feelings). Such discussions can easily deteriorate into a shallow swopping of anecdotes.

An effective way to improve the quality of reflective discussion is to provide a direct experience of what such a discussion can be like by 'modelling'. Modelling is simply providing a clear model or example, and shaping learners' behaviour towards this model.

Modelling is simply providing a clear model or example, and shaping learners' behaviour towards this model.

Two tutors, or two experienced learners (for example successful students from last year's course) can discuss their experience with the learners listening, or a single tutor can script or improvise a reflective monologue. The crucial features of reflection which any such modelling could contain are:

–   descriptions of events: details, being objective, asking yourself "How do I know that?", "In what ways was this experience similar/ different to others I have had?"

–   judgement: asking yourself "What was good/bad about the experience?", "What were its best/worst features?", "What went well/badly?".

–   analysis: asking yourself "Why did that happen?", "How can I make sense of that?", "How can that be explained?"

Modelling of reflection was used in the course described in **Section 5.9.** Trainee teachers were seen by the tutors as having rather stilted and unproductive reflective discussions when they reported back to each other about how their teaching had been going over the previous week. The tutors decided to give them an example of a more lively, varied and analytical reflective discussion. At the start of one session the chairs were arranged in a 'fishbowl': in this case 50 chairs in concentric circles around four chairs for the tutors. The following message was displayed on an overhead projector as the trainee teachers arrived for the session:

"For the first 10 minutes we will be discussing what we noticed about the way last week's session went, and in particular about how the different groups were operating. Please listen in."

The tutors had an open discussion (talking in rather louder voices than usual!) in which they tried to demonstrate critical and analytical reflection and to base this on what they had observed. Three weeks later the trainee

4.4 Providing substitute experiences

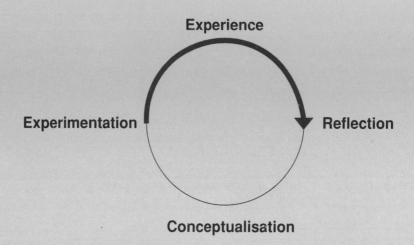

The most important implication of experiential learning theory is that active learning experiences should be provided for the learner. We are not be concerned here with the practicalities of how to provide work experience. The Further Education Unit publications **Converting Working Into Learning** and **Planned Experience** provide help in this area. The ideas in this section are about providing substitutes for direct work experience and, in particular, simulations, case studies, role plays and games.

4.4.1 Case studies

4.4.2 Games

4.4.3 Simulations

4.4.4 Role plays

4.4.5 Assessing through substitute experiences

If you were to imagine a scale which represented how real a learning situation was, and how personally involved the learner was in that situation, lectures or reading might be at one end, and direct experience of work at the other. On this scale you could place case studies, games, simulations and role plays, as in the diagram below:

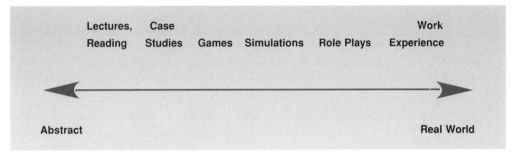

4.4.1 Case studies

A case study involves a detailed examination of a real-life or simulated situation carried out in order to illustrate special and/or general characteristics. An example might be the examination of a patient's case notes. They are useful to apply theory to practical situations, and to derive general principles from examples. A potential danger with case studies is that discussion can rush headlong to solutions without adequate description and analysis of the situation, and without exploring possible consequences of alternative solutions. The following sequence of analysis can help to structure the discussion of case studies. Stages 1 - 4 follow the experiential learning cycle from reflection to experimentation at an abstract level, without direct personal experience.

1 Understand the situation

2 Diagnose the problem

3 Create alternative solutions

4 Predict outcomes

5 Choose from among options

6 Round out the analysis

7 Communicate the results

Further reading

Easton, G.   **Learning from Case Studies** Prentice Hall, 1982.

4.4.2 Games

A game is a contest among players operating under a set of rules in order to win or to obtain a pay-off. The key feature of a game is that it involves competition. Games invariably increase learners' interest and can turn a dull topic into an exciting experience. Games also tend to help learners to loosen up and become more fully involved. The fact that it is a game gives participants permission to be lively, even silly, and allows laughter and enjoyment where this might otherwise be considered inappropriate. For this reason a game can be an effective way to start a session or a new topic on a course – loosening up attitudes and encouraging active engagement.

Some games involve elements of simulation, as with the board game Monopoly. Others involve role play, as with Dungeons and Dragons.

It can be effective to add elements of games into otherwise conventional situations: for example having teams of students competing against each other rather than simply working in parallel. An all-purpose format for this kind of game, known as the 'Game for all Seasons', involves both simulation and role play in the three stages described on page 57.

A Game For All Seasons

1   Learners are divided into teams and set the same task or problem to work on. Instead of this being merely an academic task, an element of simulation is introduced. For example, instead of Engineering Design students simply working on a design, the design task could be set in the context of an imaginary prestigious national design competition. The teams could represent different companies competing for the design prize.

2   An extra team is set up as judges of the outcomes of the team's work. While the teams get on with their work, the panel of judges discusses the criteria it will use to judge the outcomes of this work. This might be an 'Engineering Design Council'. Members of the teams could be allowed to consult the judges panel about criteria. When they did so this could be 'in role': as a member of an engineering company approaching the Engineering Design Council.

3   The teams present the outcomes of their work to the judges who question the teams and discuss the work in a 'fishbowl' (with all the teams sitting around the judges listening to the discussion but not participating). They then give their judgement and award a prize to the winning team (even a modest prize can motivate large numbers of learners for long periods).

Bringing elements of the real world in this way into what might otherwise be an unstructured and abstract discussion can have a dramatic affect on learning.

An example of the effective use of a game in what might at first appear an unpromising electrician training course can be found in **Section 5.5**.

Further reading

Ellington, H.,   **Handbook of Game Design** Kogan Page,
Addinal, E.   London. 1982.
and Percival, F.
The Game for All Seasons is adapted from a game with the same title in:

Jaques, D.   **Learning in Groups** Croom Helm, Beckenham.
                  1985.

Jaques, D.   **Learning in Groups** Croom Helm, Beckenham. 1985.

4.4.3 Simulations

A simulation represents a real situation and is continuing. A circuit diagram, although it represents actual wiring, is not a simulation because it is static. A flight simulator for training pilots is a simulation, however, because it changes with time. Simulations can come very close to reality. Computer simulations can be invaluable for studying situations which in reality are too dangerous, too time consuming, or ethically unsound. For example, it might be educationally valuable to allow an economics student to be the Chancellor of the Exchequer for five years, and elements of this experience can be achieved in an hour with the use of a computer simulation of the behaviour of the British economy. Similarly, a computer simulation of the operation of the human respiratory system allows biology students to try to keep simulated 'patients' alive by manipulating their oxygen supply in a way that would be impossible in real life. An example of this application is elaborated in **Section 5.3.**

Simulations and games can also be used as case studies: after undertaking the simulation or game, participants stop and reflect about it in order to draw general conclusions about the simulated events involved.

Further reading

Jones, K.   **Simulations: A Handbook For Teachers** Kogan Page, London. 1980.

4.4.4 Role plays

Simulations can be enriched by role play. Participants not only make decisions about what to do in the simulation, but play the role of particular individuals. An example of this in use is the 'simulated patient' technique developed at McMaster University for the training of doctors. Trainees are confronted with someone role playing a patient. Instead of simply discussing the patient's notes (a case study) they have to play the role of a doctor and talk to and examine the patient, making a diagnosis as in a real situation. This would be risky in real life, but provides an invaluable substitute for direct work experience.

As well as being used as an extra element of simulation of real life events, role playing can be used to help learners to empathise with the position and feelings of others. For example, to help sales staff to understand the feelings of frustrated shoppers, the trainee could take the role of a shopper in a simulation of a long check-out queue. This use of role play is quite common in the training of staff in areas where human relations are crucial, such as in the caring professions and in service jobs.

Role plays can be more tricky to run than case studies, games and simulations, because they involve learners personally and can arouse strong feelings and awkwardness. The following guidelines are offered to help to set up and run role plays.

Guidelines for running role plays

Role briefs
Briefs are valuable to enable inexperienced 'players' to get into a role. Briefs should not be over-elaborate or caricatures. Extreme or cliched personality traits allow too little scope for personal interpretation or unpredictability of outcomes. Too much detail makes the role too difficult to play and constrains outcomes. Briefs should contain some information about what it is reasonable for the person to know (and feel) about the other roles in the role play.

Contextual information
It is contextual information which turns a disembodied role play into a simulation role play. Such contextual information is valuable and can substitute for detail in role briefs. Some contextual information about the motives of the 'players' and the nature of the social processes or practical procedures operating can be very useful. Again, too much detail can be counter-productive. Extensive contextual information emphasises the simulation/case study aspect at the expense of personal involvement in the role play.

Scripted role plays
Scripts are useful when the purpose is to demonstrate something to the audience, or observers (as with drama), but should be avoided when it is the experience of the participants which is most important.

Observers

It is difficult for those playing roles to be observant and reflective at the same time. It is useful to nominate observers to provide the 'evidence' for subsequent discussion. Observers can use checklists : related either to general models of skill development (e.g. Carl Rogers' principles of non-directiveness) or to specific issues to do with the content of the role play. Observers can time and stop role plays. Observers can be assigned to each participant in the role play, or each can have a different observer brief. Observers can chair de-briefings.

Variations on straightforward role plays can also be used:

Time out

It can be useful if any participant can temporarily halt a role play – because he/she is stuck, distressed or wants to explore an idea immediately. All involved move to a physically separate space and discuss the issue or problem. They then return to the role play, starting either from the point at which time out was called, or from an earlier point. Time out can be used to try different ways of approaching a particular difficult moment, or to give different people the chance to role play in the same situation.

Psychodrama

Psychodrama usually involves more participants than a role play, and recreates a whole scene (e.g. a classroom) rather than an interaction between two people (though there are various kinds of personal development exercises which are also referred to as psychodramas). There is a 'director' who can call "Cut!" and freeze the action. Participants can then be 'interviewed' about their feelings, what they really want to do or say, etc. These revelations are heard in public and then the director calls "Roll!" and the action continues. Psychodrama is particularly useful for examining what is going on in a situation familiar to the person who is the focus of the drama.

Alter ego

All participants in the role play have another person standing behind them with their hands on their shoulders, acting as alter egos. The alter ego says out loud, during the role play, what he or she thinks the person is **really** thinking or feeling, e.g.:

Participant: "Oh hello! How very nice to see you!"

Alter ego: "Oh no, not him again!"

Structured de-briefing

De-briefing, the discussion which takes place after the experience of role playing, during which participants reflect on and learn from the experience, should be allocated plenty of time. A five-minute role play can easily generate enough material to keep a lively discussion going for half an hour. As participants can feel defensive about their behaviour during the role play, and can have difficulty separating their experience of the specific situation from general principles to be drawn from the experience, a structured de-briefing is recommended. This is one such structure.

1 All reflect in silence and prepare comments

2 Each role-playing participant in turn makes uninterrupted comments

3 The observers make uninterrupted comments

4 All discuss the role play

5 Participants are helped to return to 'reality' and to get out of their roles

6 All discuss general conclusions without referring to details of role play

The most important feature of de-briefing is to separate discussion of the content and experience of the role play from general discussion of what can be learnt from it. A detailed breakdown of the stages of de-briefing which follow the experiential learning cycle can be found in **Section 4.3.5.**

Further reading

Lewis, R.	**Using Role Play – An Introductory Guide** Basic Skills Unit, Cambridge. 1980.
van Ments, M.	**The Effective Use Of Role Play – A Handbook For Trainers And Teachers** Kogan Page, London. 1983.

4.4.5   Assessing through substitute experiences

Assessment tasks can also be set in the context of real situations, as with ROLE PLAY ESSAYS. Instead of simply setting conventional essays, you could set them in a simulated real life setting. For example you could:

– require electrical engineering students to take the role of the presenter of the CEGB's case for the Sizewell nuclear power station and write the 'closing speech' for the Sizewell enquiry;

– set trainee nurses the task of writing parliamentary questions for the Shadow Health Minister to ask at Prime Minister's question time about the proposed privatisation of all hospital services.

Such tasks require that the learner reflects on the simulated situation and applies knowledge to making specific plans or proposals.

Assessment tasks can also be based on substitute experiences instead of hypothetical situations, as with 'DOING IT' ESSAYS. For example, trainee teachers can be shown a brief video of a classroom in action and asked specific questions about it such as:

"Advise the teacher on alternative methods of maintaining control than those used."

"What types of questioning were used by the teacher? Suggest alternatives."

Such a task requires learners to record their experience of the video, reflect upon it in the light of their knowledge, and propose action. The task may also allow a second viewing of the video, aided by an observation schedule prompted by the first viewing and the questions, so taking the learners round the experiential cycle twice within one assessment task.

OVERVIEW

Substitutes for direct work experience are useful to:

practise skills in safe contexts

illustrate theory in action

develop interpersonal skills

increase personal involvement in learning and enliven topics

derive theory or general principles from examples

prepare learners for work experience

focus attention on experiences which are difficult or impossible to provide in any other way.

5 Case studies of the application of experiential learning methods

This section contains nine case studies selected for their illustration of experiential learning methods and practice and of the values associated with experiential learning. The case studies complement and add to the methods described in **Section 4** and methods are cross-referenced where appropriate. The ways these methods and course designs use the experiential learning cycle and experiential learning principles are highlighted.

The case studies are based on courses which the project team have taught on, have undertaken action research on, acted as consultants to or have studied. The identity of the courses has not been revealed and changes have been made in the way some of the courses have been described.

5.1   **Self-assessment of welding skills**

5.2   **Self-directed learning in office practice**

5.3   **Computer-based simulations in biology**

5.4   **A training course for new lecturers in higher education**

5.5   **"Thirty second theatre"**

5.6   **Communication skills on a Basic Nursing course**

5.7   **Self-directed development for further education lecturers**

5.8   **The use of learning journals in engineering**

5.9   **Experience-led learning on the City and Guilds 730**

5.1   Self-assessment of welding skills

At an agricultural college, students were taught the theory of a range of welding techniques in weekly lectures in a classroom. Each week they had a practical session in a workshop in which to apply the theory. These practical sessions took the following form:

Stage 1   The tutor demonstrated a welding technique.

Stage 2   Students attempted to use the technique themselves, under supervision.

Stage 3   Those students who completed the weld took it to the tutor who gave feedback on the good and bad features of the weld.

In practice there were a number of problems with this approach:

– Students paid insufficient attention to the demonstration.

– Students undertook the practical task very slowly and with little care. Some regularly failed to complete a single weld in the practical session.

– The tutor had to offer the same advice, and repeated demonstrations, to many of the students, despite a full explanation during the initial demonstration.

– A large proportion of completed welds were of a poor standard, with little evidence of students having applied a theoretical understanding of the type of weld to their practical work.

– Students seemed quite unreflective about what they were doing and why and what was going wrong. They appeared to leave it entirely up to the tutor to identify weaknesses in their welds, even when these were obvious.

– The same basic mistakes were made week after week.

In terms of experiential learning theory these problems were caused by:

– students not planning their own work or having criteria by which to judge their work, in advance;

– students not reflecting upon their work or assessing it;

– students not having the opportunity to go round the learning cycle a second time in order to correct mistakes;

– students not playing an active and responsible part in their own learning.

Faced with this situation, the tutor introduced a self-assessment process involving the following stages:

Stage 1   The tutor demonstrated the welding technique.

Stage 2   The students discussed and devised criteria for assessing the quality of a finished weld of this type. The tutor prompted with reference to the theory introduced in the lecture when necessary. These criteria were then written on the blackboard.

Stage 3   Students attempted to use the technique themselves. The tutor invited students to ask questions, especially about the implications of the criteria for techniques, but did not offer answers or demonstrations.

Stage 4   Students bent their welds to destruction and assessed their quality using the criteria they devised in stage 2.

Stage 5   Students presented their welds and their self-assessment to the tutor, giving themselves a mark out of 5 for each of the criteria. The tutor limited contributions to questions such as: "And how would you avoid that weakness next time?" to help students plan their next attempts at undertaking the welds.

Stage 6   Students repeated stages 3,4 and 5, undertaking a second weld, testing and assessing it, and presenting their conclusions and self-assessment to the tutor.

The main consequences of using self-assessment in this way were:

– Students paid more attention to the demonstration.

– Students joined in a purposeful discussion which related theory to practice in devising the criteria that they would later use themselves to assess their own work.

– Welds of higher quality, with fewer elementary errors, were produced.

– Students reflected about their own welds, and were able correctly to diagnose weaknesses using their own criteria. They were, if anything, overharsh with themselves in their marking.

– Because they worked so much faster, they had time to undertake a second weld, learning from mistakes in their first weld.

– Students planned the second weld carefully, taking into account their self-assessment of their first weld.

– Subsequent evaluation indicated that their second welds were of a consistently higher standard than their first welds, showing that they were learning from the experience of carrying out and reflecting upon their first weld.

– Students started asking more questions, during theory classes, about practical implications, such as: "What would cause a poor weld?" and "How would you avoid that kind of problem?". This change in student involvement led to a change in the nature of theory sessions from being 'chalk and talk' towards tutor-led discussions.

The main features of this innovation, in terms of experiential learning theory, are:

1 Students started with theory (**Conceptualisation**).

2 Students planned their work and devised criteria by which outcomes would be assessed and, in doing so, related theory to practice (**Experimentation**).

3 The planning stage was followed by attempting to undertake the weld (**Experience**).

4 Students tested and assessed their own work (**Reflection**).

5 On the basis of their self-assessment, they revised their ideas about how to undertake the weld (**Conceptualisation**) and planned their second weld (**Experimentation**). This gave a second opportunity for **Experience** through undertaking the second weld, and for **Reflection**, through assessing it. This took students through two complete learning cycles.

6 Students had increased opportunities to be involved responsibly throughout.

5.2   Self-directed learning in office practice

Office practice courses usually involve practice of repetitive skills, such as typing, and the development of a fairly low level of familiarity with a range of office equipment and practices. They often lead to externally set professional tests which establish levels of competence. Such courses are often provided for the 'less academic' at school or college. Teaching methods are commonly highly teacher-centred. The class moves at the pace of the slowest. Learners are usually assumed to have little or no relevant experience. Learners come to rely on the teacher for all decisions about how well they are doing, when they should move on, and so on. Almost all learning time is spent watching demonstrations and undertaking practice drills. Almost no time is spent in discussion or in reflection of any kind. Almost no time is spent on 'homework' outside class. One of the most striking things on entering a room in which office practice is being taught is that it is silent (except for the sound of typewriters) and that everybody appears to be doing exactly the same thing.

One such course at a technical college was provided for retraining. The learners on the course were not, however, 15 year olds, but mature people, most of whom had a variety of work experiences. They were also fairly independent people, used to organising their own time and establishing their own priorities. We have seen such learners submit passively to a conventional course and being treated as if they were inexperienced 15 year olds. However, in this case, the teacher used experiential learning theory to devise a different way of running the course.

The teacher wished to:

- utilise the varied work experiences of the members of the group to the full;

- negotiate the content and pace of the course with the group in order to spend time on topics where the need was greatest and to progress at an appropriate pace;

- encourage reflectiveness and self-assessment;

- establish an atmosphere which encouraged mutual supportiveness and the seeking of assistance from each other;

- mobilise enthusiasm to undertake work outside teaching sessions.

The methods the teacher used included:

1 At the end of a session, each member of the group made a 'contract' with another member to undertake a particular task in relation to the course, e.g. some shorthand practice. At the start of the next session some time was put aside to report back on what had been achieved. Anything of interest to the whole group was then briefly shared before the session got going.

2 There were frequent discussions in which progress was reviewed. In small groups, individuals took turns to say what they thought they had learnt, what they were having problems with, and what this indicated about their immediate learning needs. These needs were shared in the whole group, and decisions made about the immediate plans for the development of the course in the light of these expressed needs. This frequently led to requests to move on from a topic faster than the teacher had planned, or to spend more time on a topic which a number had found difficulty with.

3 Immediately after drill and practice exercises there would be a brief discussion in small groups in which learners asked each other for help in identifying and solving problems they were having. Learners were expected to be reflective about, for example, which T-line shorthand symbols were giving problems.

4 Learners were encouraged to discuss their experiences of learning. Tips were swopped: for example the idea of taking frequent breaks when practising motor skills such as typing or shorthand.

5 Frequent tests were offered. The purpose of these tests, however, was to provide the learners with more information with which to diagnose learning needs upon which decisions about the progress of the course were based. Many of the tests were marked by other learners. In this way they learnt to recognise errors better and came to identify these errors in their own work.

The two features which these methods share, which are almost entirely missing from many office practice courses, are:

Experimentation. Learners were frequently involved in planning what to do next: what 'homework' to set themselves, what topics to cover next on the course, when they were ready to move on, when they wanted to be tested, what to do about learning problems, and so on.

Reflection. Learners reviewed their performance and progress, and that of their peers, at every stage. They reflected on the fine details of the execution of skills as well as on their overall progress and ways of learning.

To bring about this active involvement in learning involved the teacher handing over much of the control of, and responsibility for, learning to the learners, and establishing an open atmosphere of trust and mutual supportiveness.

There were side-effects of these innovations: the room became noisy, learners progressed at different rates, sessions were relatively unpredictable and pre-arranged plans could not always be executed, some 'irrelevant' material tended to get introduced into discussions and less time was spent on straightforward drill.

However the commitment of the learners to the course, and to their own achievement, was tremendous. Progress was extremely rapid in some areas, especially those where previous experience was involved. The learners 'taught' each other a good deal. Much work was done outside formal sessions. The learners developed as learners, discovering all sorts of ways to increase the effectiveness of their efforts.

5.3   Computer-based simulations in biology

Due to technical and resource limitations, laboratory work in biology courses can become stereotyped, with students doing little more than following instructions and with little genuine experimentation. Furthermore, some biology experiments cannot be undertaken at all for various reasons:

– they take too long, such as experimenting with the growth of trees;

– they involve problems which are not amenable to experimental manipulation, such as altering the environment in a lake;

– they would be unethical, such as experimenting with human patients.

Students are denied the direct experience of active experimentation with these phenoma. All of these examples, however, are amenable to simulation on a microcomputer.

There are a number of examples of computer packages which simulate biological processes. One such package, developed at the Medical School at Manchester University, simulates aspects of human physiological processes in a sophisticated way. It is so fast and so accurate that it is used by anaesthetists in operating theatres to help them to make decisions about the air and oxygen mixture they administer to patients. A package of this kind can be used to provide biology students with substitute experiences of experimentation with, for example, human respiratory functioning.

In the Biology Department at a polytechnic, students are taught about the physiology of respiration in lectures and told how a simulation programme called MACPUFF works. This programme calculates vital measures of body functions, such as pulse and respiration rate, on the basis of calculations involving many complex biochemical reactions. When a simulated 'patient' is 'run', the program prints out detailed data about the patient every three seconds, for a minute. You are then able to change a variable (such as the percentage of oxygen in the air supply) and 'run' the patient for another minute to see what happens.

The students are posed a problem. They have to 'set up' a simulated patient on the program, with particular characteristics such as blood pressure, temperature, respiration rate, and so on. They are set the task of bringing the patient to a specified more healthy state (for example a lower pulse rate and higher blood oxygen) within a set time (for example six minutes). To achieve this the students have to manipulate some of the variables (such as the rate of respiration).

It is possible for students to devise an experiment (for example to see what happens if the percentage of oxygen is increased), run this experiment with the computer simulation, and see what happens. On the basis of the results of this experiment they could devise another experiment and carry it out, and so on. As the experiments only take a few seconds it is possible to carry out a large number very easily. It is the ease of experimentation which makes simulations of this kind so valuable.

However, this strategy would not succeed. It involves active experimentation and experience, and even some reflection on the outcomes of the experiments. But the number of biochemical reactions and variables involved is so large that such a trial and error approach is unlikely ever to lead to a workable solution, let alone to an understanding of what is going on.

To be successful the students need to refer back to their lecture notes and design experiments on the basis of knowledge of principles about the physiology of respiration. The outcomes of experiments may only make sense if the students refer to a textbook and recognise the causes of the effects created in the experiment. In fact students have to go round the complete experiential learning cycle many times before they can generate a solution to the problem and manipulate the appropriate variables in an effective way. It can take students six hours and numerous trips to the library as well as dozens of experiments to succeed.

All the tutor has to do is ask the students to produce a printout of a successful intervention in the 'patient's' functioning. It is virtually impossible to produce a printout of a successful intervention by trial and error, so the tutor can be confident that the students understand the underlying physiological processes . Every student will have produced an individual solution (so copying can be easily identified) and all solutions are clearly either successful or not, making marking easy. Students can be encouraged to work together provided that each student submits an individual printout.

In terms of the experiential learning cycle this use of a simulation involves the following stages:

1 Take notes in a lecture on the physiology of respiration

2 Devise an experiment on the basis of a partial understanding

3 Carry out the experiment

4 See what the results are in terms of the condition of the patient

5 Try to interpret the results

6 Read more about particular biochemical reactions

7 Devise a further experiment to test a new idea

8 Carry out the experiment

9 See what the results are

10 Discuss these results with another student

11 Ask the tutor to explain a particular biochemical process

12 Devise a new strategy on the basis of this new understanding

13 Carry out a series of experiments to check out these new ideas

14 ... and so on, round and round the cycle.

Further reading

Fell, D.   **Computer Biogames** Oxford Polytechnic, Oxford. 1984.

5.4   A training course for new lecturers in higher education

This case study concerns a one-year part-time training course for new lecturers at a polytechic. The lecturers select eight modules from a list of fifteen on topics such as lecturing, using computers in teaching and assessment. Each module lasts three weeks and involves a total of twelve hours work. There is the opportunity for a three-hour meeting each week. The lecturers also undertake two projects which involve a practical development in their teaching on a topic of their choice. These lecturers spend most of their time over the year teaching or doing research. They tend to be academically oriented.

The course aims to influence the ways the lecturers teach, and to pave the way for a career of self-improvement as teachers. The main opportunities for learning about teaching happen outside the course during the lecturer's everyday work and the course is designed using experiential learning to link theory with practice and to make the best use of the lecturers' everyday experience. Experiential methods are employed in four main aspects of the course:

– in the design of modules

– in self-assessment of modules

– in the use of contracts for project work

– in the setting of personal development contracts for the year following the course

Modules

Each module provides a theoretical input, in the form of a specially written learning package and other resources, and requires lecturers to try out new ideas in the context of their own teaching. Each three-week module takes lecturers around the experiential learning cycle as illustrated in the diagram on page 77. Everything above the bold horizontal line in the diagram involves the lecturers' experience of teaching, while below the line involves meetings as part of the course.

On the module on lecturing, this process has the following elements:

1   Lecturers arrive with their existing experience of lectures, their existing teaching skills, beliefs and assumptions.

2   Their experience of good and bad lectures they have attended is drawn out and reflected upon and recurring themes highlighted.

3   Evidence about the effectiveness of lectures and problems with lectures are explained in a mini-lecture, and new techniques to tackle these problems are provided in a book: "53 Interesting Things To Do In Your Lectures". The mini-lecture demonstrates many of these techniques.

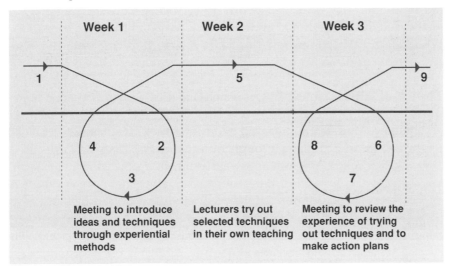

4   Lecturers choose one of the techniques from this book and try it out in their next lecture during the following week ...

5   ... gaining the experience of seeing what happened.

6   In the third week the lecturers meet to compare notes on what happened when they experimented with new techniques.

7   Further generalisations about lecturing are generated, leading to..

8   ... plans for further informal experiments in their lecturing techniques and ...

9   ... further experiences in their lectures. This experimentation can also lead on to more extensive project work later in the course.

Self-assessment of modules

Eight modules have to be 'satisfactorily completed' for lecturers to pass the course. Lecturers assess themselves, being in the best position to decide whether or not they have met the module requirements satisfactorily. They submit a self-assessment form after having completed sections which ask: "What have you done on this module? " and "What have you not done?" The learning package for each module is quite specific about what tasks are to be completed. It is common for the lecturers to do more than required, but not neccessarily the same tasks as specified. This review of their achievements gives them the evidence on which they base their decision to pass themselves, fail themselves or refer themselves. It is not all that common for lecturers to fail themselves outright, but they quite frequently refer themselves, specifying what further activities they should undertake before they could pass themselves. When they have completed this extra work they resubmit the self-assessment form.

The use of self-assessment in this way has had two main consequences:

– Standards have been improved and more work has been undertaken: the lecturers have been far tougher on themselves than the tutors used to be before self-assessment was introduced.

– Lecturers have paid more attention to module requirements and have set themselves informal criteria for what they believe would constitute an acceptable outcome from each module. They monitor their own performance throughout modules and catch up on necessary work later without any prompting from the tutors. It used to take endless nagging to get work completed.

Contracts in project work

Lecturers have to complete two projects involving modifications to their teaching. Practical projects of this kind have great potential for learning by doing but this potential is not always realised. There used to be problems at three stages in this project work:

–   At the stage of deciding what to do the tutor was often unclear what the lecturer really had in mind or whether it would be sensible, appropriate or adequate. Disagreements occcured at a later stage over what had been agreed. In attempting to 'veto' project ideas which seemed unsuitable, the tutor sometimes only succeeded in encouraging an instrumental approach in staff who then completed projects merely to meet the tutor's requirements instead of meeting a learning need of their own.

–   Modifications to projects often needed to be made for practical reasons. It was difficult deciding what changes were permissible and difficult to remember what changes had been agreed.

–   Assessment was made by the tutor. The lecturers sometimes knew that they were submitting poor work but either tried to hide this from the tutor or hoped for collusion in passing it regardless of its quality. Failing people who believed they had fulfilled an agreed proposal was virtually impossible.

This unsatisfactory situation was due in part to the lecturers not taking sufficient responsibility for the establishment of goals and criteria at the outset or for implementing these criteria on completion. They were insufficiently involved at the stage of planning for their project activities or in reflecting upon them afterwards, and this reduced the learning potential of the projects as well as causing practical difficulties. This tutor-centred assessment system was replaced with a learner-centred system with two main features:

Project agreement forms

After discussion with the whole group and the tutor, the lecturer completes a project agreement form containing two main sections entitled: 'What I intend to do' and 'What the product will look like'.

This agreement is signed by both tutor and lecturer as a 'learning contract' (see **Section 4.1.6**) on the understanding that if it is fulfilled then the lecturer will pass the project. Any amendments to the project have to be agreed by both the tutor and lecturer and added to the form.

Self-assessment

When submitting the completed project, lecturers acompany it with a self-assessment form which lists:

> Strong features of the project............
> Weak features of the project............
> Ways the project could be improved..........
> What I would like comments on.............

The tutor reads and comments on the project in the light of this information and returns it. The lecturers then pass themselves, fail themselves or refer themselves, specifying what they would need to do to justify subsequently passing themselves. They use their own self-assessment comments and the tutor's comments to justify the decision they have taken.

This process involves the lecturers in more analysis of what learning tasks will be undertaken and what will constitute an acceptable outcome and then involves them in reflection and judgement about the outcomes of their project work. In practice lecturers started to set themselves unrealistically ambitious goals, well beyond the expectations of external examiners, which the tutor had to negotiate down to something more manageable. Lecturers were also more honest, analytical and rigorous in their self-assessment, freeing the tutor to concentrate on giving useful feedback instead of trying to justify a pass or fail decision.

Personal development contracts

Once the one-year course is over the lecturers receive far less help and support in developing their teaching. A system of personal development contracts was therefore introduced in an attempt to maintain the momentum of learning by doing which had been built up over the year.

At the end of the year lecturers review their teaching through brief exercises and checklists and draft a list of development goals for themselves for the following year. Then the lecturers from the previous year's course are invited in to review the progress they have made in achieving their own development goals from a year ago, and the group listens to these reports. The lecturers then discuss their draft goals, suggesting changes and additions to each other. Finally they write out a full 'contract' in the form: "I contract with the group to ....". The tutors join in this process as well and share their personal goals with the group. These contracts have taken various forms but usually contain the following headings:

Teaching
Research/consultancy
Scholarship/reading/conferences
Learning/skill development
Administration
Personal style
Home/personal

The tutor types up these contracts and circulates them round the group. The following year the lecturers attend the last course meeting of the year to review their achievements while the new lecturers attending the course listen.

The lecturers take this process enormously seriously. They report keeping their contract with them and referring to it frequently. They say they feel a strong commitment to the group and this is evident in the way they report back after a year. They commonly bring evaluation reports, handouts and other supporting material with which to demonstrate what they have achieved. They invariably lack any other context within which they can set personal learning goals and check up on their achievement in a supportive rather than a threatening way.

5.5 "Thirty Second Theatre"

Thirty Second Theatre is a problem-solving technique designed to enable autonomous groups to help their members to tackle work problems. It allows the group to discuss and role play problems experienced by their members. Role play techniques often require skilled facilitators to organise and handle, but this method requires no such expertise: groups who have never experienced role play can use it without help. This case study describes the method and illustrates its use in practice.

Learners are divided into groups of six. About an hour is needed for each individual in the group to obtain help on his or her own work problem: about six hours in all. The learners are asked to identify a problem at work which is typical, or which highlights a particular difficulty they have. They are asked to write out this problem in the following way:

"Whatever sort of problem you have in your work, write it out in the form of a thirty second play. Your play should have a description of the scene in which the problem arose, thumbnail sketches of the main characters and thirty seconds of dialogue to get the action rolling. This play should aim to give a vivid impression of the situation you find yourself in."

The problem presented as a thirty second theatre reproduced below was written out by a music teacher who had never been involved in problem solving or group work before.

Problem: *Maintaining the students' interest and concentration can be quite a problem. Although one or two students are keen to participate in group activities, the others sometimes seem to drift off into worlds of their own. As the students all have a visual handicap, visual stimulation is impossible so I need to try and employ other strategies to hold their concentration.*

Scene: *In the music room, at college. Tutor has explained and demonstrated the playing of various rhythms and has now asked the students to do the same on their own choice of instrument.*

Characters:

Leon	student, 19, partially sighted, overweight, cheerful character, keen to please but does not enjoy group activities.
Ian	student, 18, blind, plays piano well, bright and breezy, gets frustrated at other students' lack of musical ability.
David	student, 18, partially sighted, has outbursts of temper at times and feels everyone is against him.
Tracey	student, 17, blind, very polite and well-mannered but appears to find it difficult to concentrate. Tutor finds it difficult to assess her progress as she is very quiet.
Judy	Tutor

Script

Judy	"OK, who'd like to play a waltz rhythm first?" (Long silence) "Ian, would you demonstrate a waltz rhythm please?"
Ian	"Yeah" (Demonstrates rhythm on the piano)
Judy	"David, would you like to try that on the tamborine?" (Silence at first as David is poking his finger in Leon's thigh)
David	(Sighs heavily) "OK" (Demonstrates rhythm)
Judy	"Tracy, your turn now."
Tracy	(Stirs, had nodded off to sleep) "What was that Judy?"
Judy	"Could you show us how to play the waltz rhythm?"
Tracy	"I'll try." (Bangs tamborine violently five times)
Leon	"That's not right, is it Judy?" (Slyly poking his finger in David's side)

to present their problems to the group and enlist their help in working on the problem. They are offered alternative ways of tackling the problem. Role plays may be perceived as 'risky' by those not used to them and so 'safer' discussion methods are offered as well. The method is chosen by the person whose problem is being worked on. In practice, groups tend to start off with the discussion methods and move on to 'riskier' methods as they become more confident and trusting of each other. Even totally inexperienced groups become quite experimental and imaginative in their problem solving after a few hours, working together, running role plays through over and over with different members in the key roles and so on, without prompting or help.

One set of alternative problem-solving methods could be:

Open discussion

The problem is presented to the group who have an open discussion about what it really consists of and what might be done about it. A checklist of questions can be offered to help groups who get stuck. For example:

> "How do you feel in this situation? How do the others feel?"

> "Can you state the problem from the point of view of the others?"

> "What are you most afraid might happen?"

Pyramid discussion

As for 'Open discussion' but first of all:

> Each person spends five minutes alone reflecting about the problem and making notes about possible causes.
> Pairs form to compare notes and discuss possible solutions for ten minutes.

In this way everyone in the group will have had time to think about the problem and work up some ideas before being expected to join in a group discussion.

Brainstorming

Brainstorming is a method for throwing out as many ideas or solutions to problems as possible. Before the group starts, allow five minutes to clarify what the problem is for which possible solutions are being dreamt up. Appoint a scribe who will write down the ideas as quickly as possible, preferably on a board everyone is sitting around. Appoint a referee who will call "foul!" every time someone breaks one of the three rules below. Everyone then simply calls out possible solutions to the problem, being as imaginative as possible.

Rules:

1   No elaboration: group members simply call out a word or phrase, however daft or nonsensical it may seem to others. Explanation comes later.

2   No clarification: group members may not ask what others mean.

3   No criticism: no one is allowed to criticise or comment: this would stop others from throwing out half-formed ideas.

After this fast creative stage, the group goes back through the list of ideas on the board to check what they mean, and then selects the most fruitful for further analysis.

Role play

Members of the group take the role of the characters in the thirty second theatre and read the scripted section before improvising what happens next. The group may need to be imaginative about the room layout, about other characters involved, and about how the scene unfolds. The rest of the the group observe and take notes. The purpose of the role play is for group members to experience what it is like for the characters in the problem situation before they discuss possible solutions.

Instructions for running role plays and de-briefing and reflecting upon them can be found in **Section 4.4.4**. together with additional role play techniques such as 'Time Out' and 'Alter Ego'.

Before the group finish with one problem and move on to the next, each person in the group makes a very brief statement about what they have learnt.

Thirty second theatre was used in the context of the course described in **Section 5.9**. The working methods were demonstrated at the start by the tutors acting them out so as to give learners the experience of seeing the methods in action. Five parallel problem-solving groups then worked quite independently in three rooms for six hours spread over two weeks. The method generated a tremendous amount of involvement and energy despite the lack of experience of the groups with this kind of working method. The course evaluation showed that 97% agreed or strongly agreed with the statement "I learnt a great deal from the group problem solving", the highest rating of any aspect of the course. Entries in learners' diaries also revealed the powerful impact this had on them.

In terms of experiential learning theory the effectiveness of this method was due to:

– learners identifying their own learning needs by reviewing their work experience and identifying issues of personal relevance

– the definition of problems in terms of situations and experiences rather than in an abstract way

– the use of group methods which involved learners actively

– the use of group methods which provided participants with substitute experiences of the problems being addressed

– the use of group methods which took learners round the experiential learning cycle, from problem definitions, through experiences, reflection and analysis to action plans

– the 'ownership' of the problems by individuals and their groups

– the control groups had to work in as safe or as risky a way as they dared.

5.6 Communication skills on a Basic Nursing course

Part of the first year of a Basic Nursing three-year degree programme involved a course in communication skills. The course included interviewing and counselling skills and one of its aims was to increase the student nurses' confidence in communicating with others whilst on the 15 weeks of clinical placements which interspersed the first year.

The course drew on students' placement experiences to integrate theory and practice. Almost the only 'communications theory' on the course was developed in an informal way by the students themselves analysing their experiences. The following description of a session illustrates the approach taken.

On the day prior to the session the students had all been out on a community-based clinical placement. The tutor asked the students:

> "Think back to yesterday and the experiences you had on placement. I'd like you to identify one incident which you found easy: when you felt comfortable, at ease, a part of what was going on, relaxed. I'd also like you to think of a time which was difficult: when you felt uncomfortable, you wanted to leave, you felt excluded, a spare part, you felt hostility towards you or felt unwelcome."

The students were given ten minutes for this. There were no 'ground rules' requiring students to make notes or not talk to each other (though time for silent reflection prior to discussion can be very useful at this stage). Students then described their experiences to each other. Again there were no ground rules, except to *be descriptive* rather than trying to leap to solutions. If unstructured sharing like this doesn't work well you can introduce methods such as giving each student in turn five minutes during which the other student in the pair just listens and doesn't comment.

One student from each sub-group was then asked to draw up a table:

Good situations	Bad situations

While the other students contributed to the sub-group by recounting their individual experiences, this student recorded some of the key points on this table.

The role of the tutor in this discussion was to:

– pick out 'things students all come up against'
– balance negative with positive experiences (students found it easier to remember bad experiences)
– help the sharing to be constructive rather than destructive
– help students to try to reach personal solutions to the difficult situations
– help students to rehearse solutions.

The methods used at this stage included taking a specific situation, such as coping with an unhelpful supervisor on placement, and undertaking a role play. The tutor might say: "You play the difficult supervisor and I'll show you what I might do". Instead of offering direct advice this would be demonstrated experientially. Such role plays might involve several students and even props and setting the room or furniture up as in the real situation (see **Section 4.4.4** for ideas on using role play). Students would be encouraged to generate ideas for the sorts of strategies which could be used next time they found themselves in that situation. These would be illustrated with specific examples. The following week some time would be spent exploring how the student coped when confronted with the same situations again.

There was an emphasis on specific experience and a deliberate avoidance of theory building and generalisations because the students, especially the 18 year olds, were used to working in academic ways. They preferred to deal with problems in an abstract way rather than through examining their own experience and were not so good at gaining access to their feelings and exploring these.

Charge Nurses reported very positively on students who had experienced this approach to communication skills. For example: "The students show much greater self-confidence. When they come on to the ward, instead of hiding in the office they go straight to the patients and talk to them."

Assessment of students on the communication skills course highlighted one of its problems. Initially assessment involved students writing an essay and doing a classroom test. This was obviously inappropriate and was replaced by a more applied task. Students were asked to make a video of a meeting involving specified roles and were asked to write a report analysing the communications involved. It emerged that there was insufficient briefing for how to undertake this task. Also, in the absence of a clear model of communication, students found it difficult to know what to analyse or how, and the tutors found students' reports difficult to mark in the absence of clear criteria. Subsequently the students were asked to provide an audiotape of themselves undertaking some counselling so that the emphasis was more on their skills than on their ability to analyse.

In terms of the experiential learning cycle, the typical session, exemplified in the example above, started with students reflecting (**2**) back on experiences prior to the session (**1**). These reflections sometimes led to experimenting with new ways of behaving in the form of role plays (**3**) providing new experiences (**4**), further reflection (**5**) and plans for future action (**6**). Sometimes students would carry out these plans (**7**) and report back the following week (**8**).

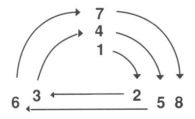

The diagram shows clearly the links made in the course between experimentation and planning, action and reflection. It also shows the way in which conceptualisation was missed out in the learning cycle. It was a lack of conceptual models which caused difficulties with the assessment.

A danger with using the experiential cycle in this way is that learners do not have a basis for generating solutions to new problems, but have to tackle each new situation as if it were unique. The next stage of development of this course will involve searching for and adopting a clear model of the communication process to form a basis for analysis of reflections on experience. This would complete the learning cycle and help students to link their experience to theory in a way which developed an understanding of the communication process as well as developing competence in specific situations requiring communication skills.

5.7 Self-directed development for further education lecturers

This is an example of a course which uses action learning (see **Section 4.1.7**). The teachers on this in-service course, which leads to a Certificate in Education for Further Education, spend one day a week on the course and the other four days with a regular teaching timetable.

The values and assumptions which underlie this course are very different from those of a teacher-centred course where the content and process is specified for the learners, and where the learners make few if any decisions about the operation of the course. To help the teachers on this course adjust to the very different responsibilities they have as learners, these assumptions are spelt out at the start of the course and the central assumptions· are reproduced below. These assumptions could act as a model for courses based on the experiences and needs of learners.competence in specific situations requiring communication skills.

The main activities on the course consist of:

Small group work (known as 'learning groups') in which individuals are given equal group time to reflect upon and discuss issues which concerned them: either about their teaching outside the course, or about their own learning on the course. These groups are stable throughout the course and meet for one hour a day.

Small group work (known as 'task groups') in which individuals form working groups to address particular shared problems.
Individuals negotiate their own groups or might even work alone. The membership of groups changes and groups dissolve and re-form as problems are solved and new issues are identified. The bulk of all available time is spent in these 'task groups'

ASSUMPTIONS, VALUES AND BELIEFS

Adults learn best when they:

1 BECOME AUTONOMOUS, that is, they move from a state of dependency to one of interdependency and autonomy.

2 MAKE USE OF THEIR EXPERIENCE, that is, we should try to take account of each course member's reservior of experience.

3 REFLECT UPON EXPERIENCE. This may require an initial unfreezing and learning to learn from experience.

4 ARE PRESENT-ORIENTED, that is, that course members' interests are centred on the present. They look for immediate application and are less willing to wait for benefits.

5 LEARN FROM PROBLEMS RATHER THAN FROM SUBJECTS. There should be an emphasis on tackling problems and issues grounded in the professional practice of course members rather than on the teaching and learning of 'subjects'.

6 ARE ACTIVITY BASED. Course members should be helped to move from passivity to activity in their approach to learning.

7 ARE INVOLVED IN NEGOTIATION. Overall the learner should accept a share of the responsibility for planning, operating and evaluating the course.

8 FOCUS ON PRINCIPLES. There needs to be a move away from an initial focus on particular experience to a focus on general principles.

9 HAVE RESPONSIBILITY FOR THEIR OWN LEARNING.

10 ACKNOWLEDGE THE IMPORTANCE OF PROCESS. Course members should reflect on their own and their group's learning processes.

11 SHARE IDEAS AND FEELINGS.

12 EXPERIENCE OPENNESS, TRUST AND COMMITMENT. There should be an emphasis on the development of equality, mutual trust and respect and mutual helpfulness.

13 SET THEIR OWN GOALS. Each course member should derive his or her own learning goals from practice.

14 ARE IN A CLIMATE CONDUCIVE TO LEARNING. A major role for the tutor is in establishing a climate conducive to learning.

The teachers are expected to examine critically their practice as teachers, identify aspects of their practice which, if improved, would enhance the learning of their students, and make a commitment to improve that aspect of their practice. The course requirement is that the teachers:

1 Write a statement describing what aspect of your current practice you want to improve.

2 Write statements describing ways (imagined) that you might improve the aspect of your practice which you have chosen to improve.

3 Write statements describing how you will know when the aspect of your practice you have chosen has improved.

The teachers are told:

Improvement of your classroom practice can be achieved through a process of continual monitoring which can be viewed as a cyclical process involving the four stages of planning, action, observation and reflection. These elements can be shown diagrammatically as follows:

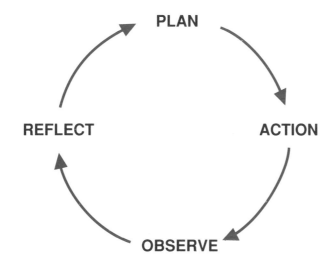

The role of the tutor on this course is explained to the teachers in the following way:

> "My job will be to facilitate your learning as you work through successive cycles, by making available resources that you need. You must see me only as a resource which you may choose to use if you feel it to be appropriate."

To help to organise and co-ordinate the independent work of the 'learning groups' and 'task work groups', the tutor sets up an additional group known as a 'community group' which is effectively the whole group. It meets at the start of every course day and runs and evaluates the course, the organisation of extracurricular activities and the planning of the content of the task work groups. This operates as a learning cycle within a learning cycle, learning about and developing the main learning processes of the course.

5.8   The use of learning journals in engineering

This case study is concerned with the way learning journals are used on an engineering degree course at a university. The course context, which itself involves experiential methods, is outlined, and the way the learning journals are used is described. But the main value of this case study is a set of advice to journal writers which was generated by the students themselves.

The course context

The learning journals are used as part of an interdisciplinary course which runs alongside eight parallel specialist science and engineering courses which students take in their first year. The purpose of this interdisciplinary course is to focus on the learning and communication processes taking place in the rest of the engineering course. There is no fixed syllabus and the topics which are covered arise out of students' identification of their learning needs and include processes such as: explaining, problem solving, reasoning, testing hypotheses, analysis, evaluation, setting and using criteria, and improving group processes.

The course employs a cyclical process based on the experiential learning theory involving three stages of reflection:

1   *The identification of learning needs* from past experience, which leads into an exploration of the chosen topic through experiential methods.

2   *Introspection* about the topic to form a sharper definition of what has been learnt and what remains, which leads into a consolidation of learning.

3   *Appraisal* of learning, comparing aspirations with achievements, which identifies areas for future learning and unresolved learning needs.

(This process is described in: **To Each According To His Needs**, Garry, A.M. and Cowan, J. Aspects of Educational Technology Vol. XXI. Kogan Page. 1986.)

The journal

This interdisciplinary course involves three hours of class activities each week, spread over two days. Reflection is a crucial aspect of the three stage learning process, and on the evening of the second day students write an entry into a personal learning journal. This entry summarises what the learner has learnt and is thinking about or has identified as personally significant or what is unresolved about the topic which has been tackled. The journal is immediately submitted to a tutor who acts as a commentator: questioning, suggesting and commenting, but never judging, correcting or directing. The purpose of the comments is to encourage further reflection. The journals are handed back very quickly so that the learning issues are still very much alive for the students. In practice the students pick up and read the comments immediately they are available, often spending more than an hour going through them carefully and thinking more about what is in the journal. This often leads to further entries in the journal.

There is no exam on the course but the journal is taken in at the end of the year and assessed in terms of the quality of effort and reflection indicating the degree of engagement of the student with the course. This quality is not possible to fake.

The students gradually become very adept at using their journals to help them to identify their learning needs and problems, to reflect on these and to identify ways forward. But at the outset they can have a lot of difficulty getting to grips with what they are for and how they can be used. Students with science backgrounds are often poor at expressing themselves in writing and may be unused to focussing on human processes instead of scientific content. These are some of the problems students encounter:

– How do you get going?

– Who is the real audience? Some write for their tutor, some write to themselves, and some write to the journal itself, as in 'Dear diary...'

– Should learning journals be organised and conclusive, or is it all right for them to be spontaneous and rambling?

– How personal, and personally revealing, should the journal be?

A small group of these engineering students were interviewed as they read through their tutor's comments on their journals in order to explore what they wrote and why, and what responses from the tutors were useful. Afterwards they joined in a brainstorm to generate advice to other students about how to get the most out of writing a learning journal. The students then shared out the ideas which were generated in the brainstorm and wrote up notes on each. Finally a collection of tidied up notes was circulated for comments. The advice which emerged is reproduced on pages 98 – 101.

ADVICE ON WRITING A JOURNAL

Starting off

If you have trouble getting going in writing your journal:

- start 'off the top': writing about whatever is at the top of your mind, regardless of whether it immediately seems very relevant or likely to be productive;

- tell an anecdote about the topic, describing an incident related to the topic, even if you aren't sure where it will lead you.

Once you have got going, ideas will tend to lead on to other ideas and before you know it you will be into your journal.

Think about good and bad, strengths and weaknesses

A good way to get started in thinking and writing about your experiences and ideas is to list what is good and what is bad about them, for example what is good and bad about a design. Alternatively you can list your strengths and weaknesses on the topic:

"What I understand well.....what I understand badly"

"What I'm good at.........what I'm bad at"

"What went well........what went badly"

Use simple English and clarify what you write

Avoid mumbo-jumbo, waffle or vocabulary which is not easily understood. Try to use simple English: that makes you realise exactly what you meant when you review your journal. And the audience (whoever they are) should be able to understand it easier too!

Aim for a well-structured journal: summarise points and repeat for emphasis and clarity if necessary.

Refer to the previous journal entry

A good starter for a journal entry is to refer back to your tutor's comments on your previous journal entry. Read them and check you understand them:

– Do you agree with the comments?

– Can you answer the questions?

By setting out to answer these outstanding questions you will find that the new journal entry has a definite structure.

Be yourself

Write down your own thoughts and feelings. Don't copy them from someone else. Be honest. If you make things up or engage in wishful thinking this won't help you, nor will the comments you get back from your tutor.

Remember that the journal is for you to explore **your** feelings and concerns **your** development. You can only learn from your journal if you have enough courage to face yourself as you really are.

Don't worry about the reactions of your tutor while you are writing

Don't change your thoughts or feelings in any way. Write exactly what you want and don't think about the comments you might get back.

Be positive

Think about what emerges from experience which is positive, productive and useful - how else will you make progress?

Decide who you are writing for

It may help you to write for a specific person or audience: a friend, your parents, even your tutor. This allows you to give direction to your thinking. But this may also intimidate you and inhibit you from revealing your feelings and thoughts. The best readership to write for may be yourself!

Keep probing

Urge yourself to keep digging deeper and deeper so that you can understand and use your understanding. Try to work towards:

– 'truths' you have discovered through your experiences;

– advice to yourself about what to do in the near future;

– finding questions which you need to think about next, about issues which you don't yet fully understand but need to understand.

Deal with it in bits and pieces

Break whatever you want to say or think about into separate topics. Deal with them one at a time, in an order that makes sense to you. Then think about how, if at all, they fit together. Or follow that sequence the other way, starting with an overview and then concentrating on each bit, one at a time.

Pinpoint where it all began

You will find it very difficult to think about thinking and to report that in a journal. Try to identify the incidents from which your thinking began. Write about them a little, describe them, enough to explain why they made you think. And then report (in one sentence if you possibly can) what it is that you were thinking about.

Explore your opinions

Have no reservations about saying what you feel or think, even if you can't explain why or don't know why. That can be a good starting-point. It may be a week or two before you begin to find the answer. If you start asking "Why?" of yourself the process of enquiry will begin at the back of your mind.

Don't restrict yourself to words to describe your thinking

Some of us find it much easier to sum up our thinking in models or diagrams or even in sketches. If that's your way, then it is probably the best way for you. You should certainly follow it when you are 'writing' your journal. But make sure that you can explain what your pictures and diagrams mean and that you are not just using them to avoid preciseness and rigour.

Generalise

None of the effort you put into your journal will be of any use unless you can turn away from the specific situations in which your thinking started and find conclusions, or advice, or queries, which are of general relevance to you.

Make plans

The easiest way to write a journal is to philosophise: writing general statements which review a week of activity but which don't really help you to make any personal progress.

Push yourself to move on to an action plan for next week (or next year!). Push yourself to spell out that action plan in simple, relevant, practical steps: steps that you can follow. Try to discipline yourself to go back, a week later, and see if the action plan worked, and if not, why not. There is no point in keeping a journal unless it helps you to develop and do better next time.

Talk to other students

When you find the task difficult, talk to other students in your class and it will probably reassure you to discover that they are meeting the same kind of difficulties as you are.

If you are not confident of the value of a new and strange experience, talk to students in the year above you. They'll be able to tell you how they got on and whether or not the experience has been worthwhile in the long term. They will probably also have some useful hints and suggestions. And students are much better at advising other students than lecturers are because students can remember what it was like when they were in your position.

This advice was generated by four students: Paul Grant, Kathryn Evans, Keith Frazer and Ian Watt, with the help of their tutors, John Cowan and Derek Fordyce. A fuller version of this advice, together with advice from students to tutors who comment on journals, is available from Derek Fordyce, Department of Civil Engineering, Heriot-Watt University.

5.9   Experience-led learning on the City and Guilds 730

City and Guilds 730 is an initial training course for teachers in adult and further education. This case study concerns one term of this course consisting of nine three-hour sessions. The constraints faced by this course were considerable and might in some circumstances have deterred innovation:

–   City and Guilds specifies a syllabus in some detail.

–   There were 55 teachers on the course: a large group with which to use experiential methods.

–   The teachers came from very varied backgrounds and had a wide range of qualifications. Some had no experience of teaching whilst others had been teaching for a number of years. They taught a wide variety of subjects, from computing to karate, and those they taught had a wide range of abilities and needs.

–   The classroom available was not conducive to learning: gloomy, scruffy and depressing with broken furniture and shabby old posters on the walls.

–   The course ran in the evening from 6pm – 9pm after the teachers and their tutors had already completed a day's work.

Conventional didactic knowledge-centred methods were useless in this context: the variations in background knowledge, skills and interests of the learners were too great, and the motivation problems too acute. An experience-based programme was devised to tackle these constraints which involved active learning and a clear link between what took place on the course and the teachers' teaching experiences during the week between sessions. Six elements of this course are described here:

- The explicit use of the experiential learning cycle to sequence course elements.

- The use of learning logs for teachers to record their reflections on teaching-based tasks.

- The use of experiential methods during classroom sessions.

- The use of problem groups.

- The use of a learning review at the end of the course.

- Evaluation evidence concerning the outcomes of the course.

Use of the experiential learning cycle

At the first session experiential learning theory was introduced to the group. They completed a learning styles inventory to identify their own preferred learning style (see Section 3). It was stressed that the most important learning opportunities would take place not on the course but in their everyday teaching, and that the course was designed to help them to make the best use of this opportunity by:

- helping them to identify their own learning needs, to reflect upon their practice and increase awareness of their experience;

- helping them to share experiences and make sense of them;

- supporting risk taking and experimentation, including creating a supportive climate;

- offering new concepts with which to analyse their teaching and new methods to try out in their teaching.

The main process of the course was explained to them using the diagram on page 104.

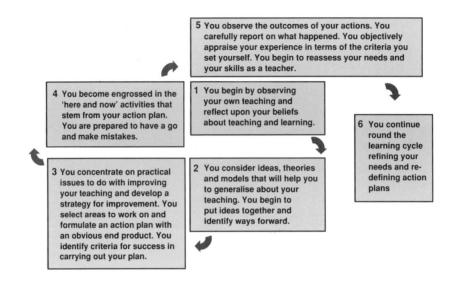

At several points in each session the group were reminded which stage they were currently at on the cycle and what the next steps would involve.

The use of learning logs

The teachers were each given a ring binder for their handouts and notes. Each week the class-based exercises were supported by worksheets and checklists which the teachers filled in and added to their ring binder. Each week they devised for themselves an action plan, based on the concepts introduced that week, which involved them trying out something in their teaching and/or reflecting upon what happened in one of their classes. Their notes on this reflection also went into their ring binder which built up into a learning log. The log became a record of their thoughts and feelings and a resource for future development of their teaching. The teachers handed in their learning log for assessment at the end of the term: the logs provided the best indication of the quality of the teachers' engagement with the course.

Observation and reflection tasks were undertaken in sessions in order to develop the skills necessary for similar observations and reflections outside the class. For example, the first activity for the learning log involved watching a short video of a lecturer giving a conventional lesson. An observation sheet asked the teachers to identify helpful things the lecturer has probably done in preparation for this lesson, and helpful things the lecturer did during the lesson. Small group discussion and a brief plenary session illustrated the range of things which could be observed and thought about and provided a model for the teaching-based activity to be undertaken over the following week. This involved a handout with instructions and headings as in the example on page 106.

At the start of the next week's session the teachers met in small groups (the same groups each week in order to build up trust) to share and discuss the outcomes of this activity in their learning logs.

This activity may seem rather simple and lacking in theoretical content, but the teachers were quite unused to oberving themselves and reflecting on their own teaching and some found even this activity difficult. As the course progressed the teaching-based activities became more demanding, the observations more specific and subtle, and the reflections more sophisticated and analytical, based more closely on conceptual frameworks offered during the sessions.

Reflections on your own teaching

After teaching a lesson, write a short account of what took place. Do this as soon as possible after the end of the lesson. At this stage don't attempt to evaluate the lesson or your teaching performance; concentrate instead upon what actually happened.

Now try to categorise your observations. Use the following headings:

Things I did before and during the lesson which should have helped my students to learn.

Any unplanned things I did during the lesson which should have helped my students to learn:

Finally write a brief statement of this work describing:

What insights, if any, I gained into the ways in which I helped my students to learn.

The use of experiential methods in sessions

Even when the content of the course might normally have been handled in a didactic way, experiential methods were employed in order to involve the teachers actively and operationalise the ideas involved. For example:

— A session on demonstration involved a tutor showing one of the teachers how to use a polaroid camera whilst the whole class observed and took notes on the methods used. They then compared notes, discussed demonstration techniques in general, and selected a technique they could use in their own teaching.

— A session on motor skill training involved dividing the class into threes. One person taught a second how to do half knots and flat knots in macrame whilst the third person observed using a brief checklist (see **Section 4.1.4** for an example of an observation checklist). The observers then reported back to the whole group on what they had seen and which training techniques seemed successful.

— A session on games and simulations involved all the teachers playing a simulation game called 'San Leona' which was used to illustrate many of the design features of games and to demonstrate their capacity for intense involvement of learners.

Learning activities, games, demonstrations, videos and exercises were used at every opportunity. These activities were followed by reflection, analysis and the planning of application of the ideas to the teachers' own teaching, rather than expecting learning to take place on the basis of abstract conceptualisation alone.

The use of problem groups

Two weeks of the course were devoted to problem solving in groups. The teachers identified problems in their own teaching which they wanted help with and formed groups. The groups then used a technique called 'thirty second theatre' to tackle each teaching problem in turn. The problem solving involved structured discussion, brainstorming and role play. Thirty second theatre is described in **Section 5.5**.

The use of a learning review

The last task the teachers were set outside the sessions was to review their learning logs, reflect on their teaching since the course started and to write down at least three statements to complete the sentence:

"What I have learnt about teaching and learning is ....."

The last session of the course was held in a room where flip chart paper had been stuck up all round the walls. The teachers were asked to write up their three statements on these posters. They were then asked to go round and read all the statements made by others in *silent* reflection. They could make written comments, write questions, respond to others' questions in writing, but *not speak*. This reflective review of what had been learnt was an intense experience for many and generated an enormous number of thoughtful and revealing statements and some interesting written 'debates' about unresolved issues. There was no attempt by the tutors to summarise the course for the teachers, which would have indicated a lack of respect for the teachers' unique personal summaries. Instead the tutors joined in as equal participants and added their own learning statements and commented on others' statements.

Evaluation evidence

Evaluation evidence was obtained by questionnaire, by open-ended written feedback and through interviewing.

The questionnaire showed the extent to which the teachers had taken on board the basic principles of experiential learning. A section of the questionnaire results is reproduced on page 109.

Data from the questionnaires also revealed that while all the teaching and learning methods used gained good ratings, the teachers felt they had learnt least from lectures and presentations, and most from the group problem solving, the exercises and activities, the discussion of teaching with other teachers and the activities undertaken during the week between sessions.

Questionnaire results

	strongly agree	agree	neutral	disagree	strongly disagree
Experimentation "I find myself trying new teaching methods to a greater extent"	13	12	2	2	0
Awareness of experience "I find myself noticing more of what is going on in my teaching"	23	6	0	0	0
Reflection "I find myself being more reflective about my teaching"	23	6	0	0	0
"I discuss teaching with my colleagues/friends to a greater extent"	11	15	0	0	1
Conceptualisation "I now understand better what I am doing in my teaching"	12	16	1	0	0

The open-ended written feedback and statements from the learning review highlighted the value to the teachers of experiential learning and the experiential methods used:

"My most significant memory of this course is ..."

"The importance of the experiential learning cycle"

"The realisation of how important reflecting on one's teaching is."

"The value of Kolb's experiential learning cycle as an aid to learning"

"Discussing a teaching method, having a week to carry it out and discussing results"

"The between-sessions diary activities and discussion"

"Actual teaching practice and the value of sharing activities to discuss and solve problems met during it"

"The value of problem solving in a small group of fellow teachers"

"The group work was very helpful with advice for my problem and also for future problems"

"What I have learnt about teaching and learning is ..."

"Time spent on reflection and evaluation is crucial to good teaching"

"Theory does not mean a lot unless it has direct application in the workplace"

"You learn best in groups or via discussion"

The interviews revealed that values associated with experiential learning also had an impact on the teachers :

"Feelings and attitudes may be as important as knowledge"

"This course involved my feelings"

"The course has been a very personal thing for me. I have changed my attitude and have a new way of looking at things"

"The group has been great fun, very supportive and a good learning experience"

"I became able to accept criticism"

"By creating a safe environment for students, learning may be increased"

6 Learning to use experiential methods

This section is designed to enable any group of teachers or trainers to run workshops for themselves in order to introduce themselves to experiential learning theory and methods. Five workshops, each lasting from one to three hours, are described, complete with instructions, materials and detailed timings. The programme for a one-day training event, constructed from these workshops, is also outlined.

The section also summarises some assumptions about how teachers and trainers can change and adopt experiential learning methods, and contains a list of common problems which are encountered when introducing experiential methods into otherwise conventional courses.

6.1 Assumptions about using experiential learning methods

6.2 Problems with experiential learning methods

6.3 Advice on running the workshops

6.4 Workshop 1: Learning sequences and experiential learning

6.5 Workshop 2: Learning styles

6.6 Workshop 3: Teaching and learning methods for experientia! learning

6.7 Workshop 4: Case studies in experiential learning

6.8 Workshop 5: Course design for experiential learning

6.9 Experiential Learning: A one-day workshop

6.1 Assumptions about using experiential learning methods

The ideas, methods and case studies in this guide are offered within a framework of assumptions about how teachers and trainers develop and change in their methods:

1   The process of change itself involves the experiential learning cycle. We see teachers reflecting on problems they experience in their courses, thinking about experiential learning ideas, selecting experiential learning methods and trying these out, observing the consequences and so on in an action research process. This can be difficult to achieve on your own. Just as this guide was written through co-operative action research, so teachers can co-operate together to share their plans and experiences. Regular meetings with a colleague or a group are likely to provide vital support, encourage more risk taking and enrich reflection and learning about the use of experiential learning methods.

2   Different trainers and teachers will have different styles, and will emphasise different aspects of the experiential learning cycle in the methods they use. To some extent we see trainers experimenting with methods which emphasise aspects of the cycle which they do not normally emphasise. For example an academic who normally stresses conceptualisation through lectures and set reading might experiment with more active learning methods. A trainer who normally stresses practice and practical learning tasks might experiment with more reflection about learners' experience of these tasks.

3   Learning how to use experiential methods is not an all-or-nothing business. You do not have to swallow the theory whole and abandon all your existing tried and tested methods. Changing can be an incremental process involving only as much experimentation and risk as feels comfortable and realistic.

4   Experiential learning does not have to involve real-world tasks. Just because you teach atomic physics or international politics does not mean that experiential methods are inappropriate. Experiential learning can take place at any point along a continuum from real world to abstract tasks:

Real World   **Abstract**

◄───►

5 Experiential learning does not have to involve a heavy emphasis on personal feelings, personal growth or commitment. It can take place at any point along a continuum from high personal involvement to low personal involvement:

**High personal   Low personal
involvement   involvement**

6 Experiential learning does not necessarily mean turning all the power and control over to your students or trainees. It can be important for learners to take responsibility for their learning but experiential learning can be implemented in highly structured and teacher-led ways. It may be necessary with inexperienced learners and those used to teacher-centred methods to start off with a teacher-centred approach to experiential methods and gradually move towards a learner-centred approach. Experiential learning can take place anywhere along a continuum from learner-centred to teacher-centred:

Learner-centred   Teacher-centred

7 Introducing experiential learning does not mean turning your entire course upside down. Some courses are designed around experiential learning theory and are centred on active learning experiences. But very small activities can be introduced into otherwise conventional courses. While experiential learning might involve a one-year independent project, it might also involve a five-minute reflection exercise at the end of a lecture! A concern for experiential learning can be expressed through any size of learning activity.

Long duration   Short duration

Overview

Because of the enormous range of ways of implementing experiential learning it is always possible to introduce it to some extent in any situation, whatever the constraints. Many courses have a syllabus, timetable and assessment system which are beyond the control of the individual teacher. But it is possible to start tomorrow with small, safe activities without changing your syllabus, timetable or assessment. In time you may wish to extend the scope and nature of the experiential learning elements of your courses until your aims, timetables and assessment methods need to be redrafted to reflect your new methods and the whole nature of your courses change. You may need to be involved in negotiation with colleagues, course approval bodies or validating agencies. But you don't have to start off like that. You can easily start now!

6.2   Problems with experiential learning methods

Introducing experiential learning methods is not all plain sailing. There are likely to be a number of problems and learners may take some time to get used to new ways of learning, especially when they are used to traditional teacher-centred and content-oriented methods. You may have some learning to do yourself as well. When you first gave a lecture you probably misjudged how much content to include. There are common mistakes and pitfalls to experiential learning as well. The following list is included to help you to anticipate potential pitfalls and to suggest ways of avoiding them.

Attempting too much

It can be difficult to judge how long learner activities will take and the most common problem is to try to fit in too much. Allow plenty of time for groups to form, for groups to get going on tasks and for reflection and discussion after tasks.

It is also easy to attempt too many innovations at once. Both you and your learners will take time to get used to new methods and you may compound your problems if you introduce too much too fast. You may also have trouble recognising which bits caused problems if there are too many changes at once!

Getting the balance wrong

A common mistake is to get so wrapped up in introducing active experiences that there is too little time left over for reflecting upon them and analysing and learning from the outcomes. Five minutes of role-play can easily generate 40 minutes reflection and discussion. A week-long work placement deserves a substantial block of follow-up time if its learning potential is to be exploited.

Conventional lecture-based courses often get the balance wrong in a different way: allocating almost all the available time to introducing new ideas without adequate opportunities to see what implications they have for practice or to experience these implications.

Assuming that learners are radical

Learners can be more conservative than their teachers and can resist new methods, especially methods which require more active involvement, more commitment, more responsibility and more openness. You may need to spend time explaining why you want to make changes, selling your ideas. You are likely to need to introduce changes progressively: gradually increasing the size of independent learning activities, progressively extending the role of learners in planning activities and in devising and implementing assessment schemes, and so on. Teachers need to try to understand learners' very sensible reasons for protecting their safe and undemanding world where teachers do all the thinking for them.

Having no structure

Carl Rogers, in 'Freedom to Learn', talks about freedom *within a system of constraints*. Experiential learning does not mean abandoning all responsibility for the way learning takes place and assuming that somehow learners will use their new independence in an effective way. Structure, guidelines and even clearly defined limits can be invaluable to learners in being able to grasp and use a degree of independence. Timetables, deadlines, checklists, criteria, the organisation of groups all support experiential learning. The experiential learning cycle itself imposes a powerful structure of its own. Introducing experiential learning methods involves at least as much planning as does the use of conventional methods.

Over-planning and keeping too tightly to plans

It can be helpful to have detailed plans of how sessions are expected to take place: in the absence of a lecture script or other form of lesson plan this can be very reassuring. But experiential learning can be very messy. If experiences are not to be entirely predictable then outcomes are going to be suprising and it is important to be ready to respond in a flexible way to whatever emerges. The most important learning resource you have to work with is not your own expertise or your plans but the experiences of your learners. You have to be prepared to abandon your plans if more promising opportunities arise.

Having no clear outcomes

Learning outcomes from experiential learning are not just unpredictable, they can also be hard to identify at all. Being flexible and responsive can lead to confusion and a lack of clarity about what an experience was for or what has emerged. When an imbalance has led to insufficient time being spent on reflection and analysis of experience, the point of the whole exercise may be lost.

A carefully structured de-briefing (such as that illustrated in **Section 4.3.5**) can overcome this problem. It can be useful to make sure that any planned experience is rounded off with personal statements about what has been learnt, and that there is adequate time and discussion before this to allow individuals to be able to recognise what they have learnt.

Closing down options

Experiential learning demands an openness to experience and this implies an acceptance of uncertainty: uncertainty as to what might happen, uncertainty as to what experiences mean, uncertainty as to what outcomes might look like. Some teachers find uncertainty very difficult to cope with and close down opportunities and come to premature conclusions and decisions. Some learners do this as well, as illustrated in **Exercise 2** in **Section 3**.

Undervaluing experience

Courses sometimes have active experiences built in but then operate in a knowledge-centred way which shows that they do not really value this experience. For example, an engineering degree course might contain a whole year in industry but then use an assessment system which consists entirely of three-hour written exam papers based on lecture courses. The assessment system is the clearest indication of the extent to which experience is valued and made use of, but there are other give-aways such as teachers having preprepared summaries of learners' experiences, and even telling learners in advance what they are about to experience. Students quickly recognise that their experience is not taken seriously and stop paying attention to it.

Setting an unsuitable tone and atmosphere

It would be hard to overestimate the importance of emotional issues in making experiential learning work effectively. It is easy to establish atmospheres which are too rushed, too threatening, too lacking in trust, too impersonal and insufficiently accepting of the expression and value of feelings to allow experiential learning methods to work effectively. Time spent on establishing an appropriate tone usually pays off handsomely.

Not adjusting to the group

Learners vary in the rate at which they get used to experiential learning methods and learn to use them effectively. Individuals and groups can seldom be rushed and teachers need to be patient and adjust the rate of change and innovation accordingly. It can be useful to acknowledge problems and to reflect upon these openly, moving forward when learners say they are ready.

Notes on problems you experience with experiential learning methods:

6.3   Advice on running the workshops

These workshops are designed to be run without the need for an expert in experiential learning or an expert workshop facilitator: they are 'do-it-yourself' workshops. Everyone involved takes part on an equal basis. They are completely self-contained and require no materials which are not contained in this guide.

Numbers of participants

Workshops 1, 2 and 5 are designed to operate with sub-groups of four, with much of the work being done in these sub-groups. This means that they can operate effectively with almost any multiple of four. In practice these workshops would work best, and be easiest to manage, with 12 – 40 participants.

Workshops 3 and 4 can operate with 6 – 30 participants but would work best with 10 – 16 participants.

Room layout

Workshops 1, 2 and 5 require flexible furniture enabling sub-groups of four to work together and also to allow the sub-groups to address the whole group.

Workshops 3 and 4 require informal seating in a circle.

No audio-visual aids or presentations are involved except in Workshop 5 which requires flipcharts or posters, marker pens and wall space to display the posters.

Workshop announcements

Each workshop has a full set of instructions which one participant should read out. It is also necessary for one participant to take responsibility for the timing of the successive stages of the workshop. The timekeeper simply tells the announcer when the suggested time for each stage has elapsed.

Flexibility

In line with the values of experiential learning, most will be gained from these workshops if participants take responsibility for their own learning and introduce their own modifications to the workshops in the light of their experience.

Materials

Participants should each be provided with a copy of this guide at the workshop, but not before. No other materials are necessary.

Your own notes on using these workshops:

6.4 Workshop 1: Learning sequences and experiential learning

This Workshop is based on **Exercise 1** on page 13 in **Section 2.** The exercise requires participants to take a section from a course, or a teaching or training session, for which they are responsible, and to analyse the sequence of learning activities involved in terms of the stages of the experiential learning cycle.

Stage 1 **5 minutes**	**Working individually** Read **Section 2** of the Guide, pages 9 – 14, but don't do the exercise on page 13 yet.
Stage 2 **5 minutes**	**Working in groups of four** Introduce yourselves within your group. Discuss the four stages of the experiential learning cycle with the aim of clarifying what they mean and clearing up misunderstandings.
Stage 3 **10 minutes**	**Working individually** Do **Exercise 1** on page 14. Take a section from a course, or a teaching or training session, for which you are responsible, and analyse the sequence of learning activities involved in terms of the stages of the experiential learning cycle. Use the diagram on page 14 and the space beneath it to write out your analysis.
Stage 4 **20 minutes**	**Working in groups of four** Take it in turn to explain your analyses of your courses or sessions to your group. Try to keep to the terminology of experiential learning theory. Ask yourselves whether the sequences you use follow the experiential learning cycle. Allow about 5 minutes each.
Stage 5 **20 minutes**	**As a whole group plenary** Raise issues which emerge with the whole group.

Questions which might emerge include:

At what point in the experiential learning cycle do most learning sequences seem to start and stop?
Which stages of the experiential learning cycle seem to be emphasised, and which missed out?

At which stages in the cycle are decisions made about what to do next, and who makes these decisions?"

60 minutes

Your own notes on Workshop 1:

6.5 Workshop 2 :   Learning styles

This Workshop is based on **Exercise 2** on page 18 in **Section 3.** The exercise requires participants to identify the learning style exhibited by three students on a computing course.

Stage 1
5 minutes

Working individually
Read **Section 3** of the Guide, pages 17 and 20, and do **Exercise 2** on page 18 *without looking at the suggested solution on page 19.*

Stage 2
10 minutes

Working in groups of four
Introduce yourselves to your group. Compare your answers to **Exercise 2** with those of the other participants, and with the suggested solution on page 18.

Stage 3
10 minutes

Working individually
Take an open-ended task or problem in your own subject area and imagine how individuals with each of the four different learning styles explained on page 16 might go about that task. Write these different approaches down as caricatures of extreme styles.

Stage 4
20 minutes

Working in groups of four
Take it in turn to explain your caricatures of what the four experiential learning styles might look like in your subject area. Allow about 5 minutes each.

Stage 5
15 minutes

As a whole group plenary
Raise issues which emerge with the whole group. Questions which might emerge include:

Which styles are easy to recognise and occur most often?

Which styles are most or least effective for the tasks you have discussed?

Are your learners aware of their styles? Are they flexible in adopting styles appropriate to the tasks you set?

Do the tasks you set require some styles to the exclusion of others?

60 minutes

Your own notes on Workshop 2:

6.6 Workshop 3: Teaching and learning methods for experiential learning

This workshop introduces participants to the range of teaching and training methods in **Section 4** of the guide. Although the structure of the workshop is extremely simple, it has been used to great effect with many leaderless groups and is an effective way to structure discussion and share methods.

Stage 1
2 minutes

Working alone
Select a sub-section of **Section 4** of the guide which interests you. Use the introduction on page 23 to help you to select.

Stage 2
2 minutes

Working as a whole group
Participants introduce themselves in turn to the group and state which item they have chosen and why. Those who have chosen an item already chosen by someone else should select an alternative item.

Stage 3
6 minutes

Working alone
Read the item you have chosen, making notes so that you can present and explain the item to the group in six minutes' time.

Stage 4
45 minutes

Working as a whole group
Starting with the person with the *largest feet*, take it in turns (with a maximum of five minutes for each turn) to explain to the group the item you have read. You must also chair the discussion of the use of your chosen teaching or training method which ensues. When your five minutes are up, the chair passes to the person to your *right*. Continue round the group until everyone has had a turn.

Stage 6

If the group is small (fewer than 8) and there is still enough interest and time, repeat stages 1 – 3, choosing new items.

Stage 7
5 minutes

Working as a whole group
Each person in turn, starting with the person with the *smallest nose*, makes a **short**, **positive** statement about one of the methods which has been discussed.

---

60 minutes

6.7   Workshop 4:   Case studies in experiential learning

This workshop introduces participants to the application of experiential learning methods through the case studies in **Section 5** of the guide. Although the structure of the workshop is extremely simple, it has been used to great effect with many leaderless groups and is an effective way to structure discussion and share methods.

Stage 1 **2 minutes**	**Working alone** Select a case study from **Section 5** of the guide which interests you, using the list on page 65 to help you.
Stage 2 **3 minutes**	**Working as a whole group** Participants introduce themselves in turn to the group and state which item they have chosen and why. Those who have chosen an item already chosen by someone else should either select an alternative item, or (if all items have been 'taken') join the person who has already chosen the item.
Stage 3 **10 minutes**	**Working alone (or in small groups)** Read the item you have chosen, making notes so that you can present and explain the item to the whole group in 15 minutes' time. Any small groups should work co-operatively.
Stage 4 **40 minutes**	**Working as a whole group** Starting with the person (or small group) with the *most hair,* take it in turns (with a maximum of five minutes for each turn) to explain to the group the item you have read. You must also chair the discussion of the use of your chosen teaching or training method which ensues. When your five minutes are up, the chair passes to the person (or small group) to your *right.* Continue round the group until everyone has had their turn.
Stage 6 **5 minutes**	**Working as a whole group** Each person in turn, starting with the person with the *smallest ears,* makes a **short, positive** statement about one of the case studies which have been discussed.

60 minutes

6.8 Workshop 5: Course design for experiential learning

In this workshop participants apply experiential learning theory and methods to their own courses to design new courses or sessions. Teams work co-operatively and present their plans on posters before a final review. This workshop would work best if preceded by at least one of Workshops 1 – 4. If it is being used alone then participants should each be given a copy of the guide beforehand so that they can familiarise themselves with experiential learning theory and methods.

As this is a three-hour session in which groups work independently for much of the time, groups will need to know when they should come together for the next stage and the timekeeper and announcer will have to liaise to inform them in plenty of time. It is crucial that the posters are displayed on time for stages 3 and 5.

Stage 1
10 minutes

Form working groups

Form working groups of two to five participants. Your task will be to redesign a short course, part of a course or a workshop with which you are familiar so that it embodies the values, ideas and methods of experiential learning. You will be working in your groups for two hours so make sure you make the right decision for your own learning!

Stage 2
20 minutes

Clarify your task

Discuss which aspects of experiential learning you are most keen to introduce, and what methods this might involve. If these goals matter to you and can to be implemented then you are likely to learn more than if you are only doing an abstract 'what if' exercise.

Write out on a poster the task your group is setting itself, e.g.:
> In the first year of the Urban Design Diploma:
> (i) To increase students' first-hand experience of urban design problems by introducing fieldwork.
> (ii)To encourage them to be more observant and reflective whilst undertaking fieldwork by introducing self-assessment of fieldwork tasks.

Display your poster next to where your group is working so that other groups can see what you are up to.

Stage 3
5 minutes

Tour posters
Have a look at the other groups' posters. You may get ideas to help you clarify or modify your own group's task, or you may decide to leave your own group and join another (if they will let you!). Write comments or questions on others' posters.

Stage 4
100 mins

Group work
Work in your groups to achieve your group's goal. Use the guide to help you. Call on others from other groups for help. Produce a poster to display your plans and ideas and have this finished and displayed by the time the 100 minutes are up.

Stage 5
40 minutes

Group tour of posters
The whole group attends each poster in turn. The group whose poster is being viewed takes not more than five minutes to explain it, followed by not more than five minutes of comments and questions. Try to share the time fairly between groups. Issues you might wish to raise include:

How do these plans implement experiential learning?

Which values are stressed?

What sequence(s) of learning tasks are involved?

Where is the experimentation, experience, reflection and conceptualisation taking place?

Which methods are new to you, and to the learners?

Where are problems most likely to occur?

Stage 6
5 minutes

Whole group
Stand in a large circle. Each person in turn has the opportunity to make one brief positive statement (not more than two sentences) about how experiential learning could be introduced into his or her teaching. You may 'Pass' on your turn if you wish. You may not speak when it is not your turn.

_____

180 minutes

6.9 Experiential learning: A one-day workshop

This workshop design links Workshops 1,2,4 and 5 within a '9 to 5' day. Workshop 3 can be substituted for Workshop 2 if participants are more interested in teaching and training methods than in learning styles.

The warm-up exercise can be crucial to establishing the right kind of openness to experience. A simple and safe exercise is to ask participants, in pairs, to spend five minutes each telling each other about a rich and rewarding learning experience they have had, and how that felt.

9.00	**Introduction** Explain programme. Hand out copies of the guide. Appoint an announcer and timekeeper.
9.10	**Warm-up exercise** To establish the tone for the day
9.20	**Workshop 1** Learning sequences and experiential learning
10.20	**Coffee**
10.50	**Workshop 2** Experiential learning styles
11.50	**Break**
12.00	**Workshop 4** Case studies in experiential learning
1.00	**Lunch**
2.00	**Workshop 5** Course design for experiential learning
3.30	**Tea** (Served during group work in Workshop 5)
5.00	**Close**

SCED: The Standing Conference on Educational Development

SCED was responsible, in conjunction with the Further Education Unit (FEU), for organising and running the national conference 'Learning by Doing' which launched this guide. SCED also arranges follow-up conferences and training workshops on a regional basis and within individual institutions in order that a wider audience can benefit from the content of national conferences.

If you are interested in arranging an event to introduce experiential learning methods to staff you might wish to contact SCED for advice on consultants and educational development staff to help you to design and run your event.

Contact:

Bob Farmer
Educational Development Unit
Birmingham Polytechnic
Perry Barr
Birmingham
B42 2SU

FURTHER EDUCATION UNIT

Elizabeth House, York Road, London SE1 7PH Telephone 01–934 9000

Board of Management

Chairman
Allan Ainsworth, Personnel Manager, John Player Group

Members
J Baker, Confederation of British Industry
B Barber, Trades Union Congress
J A Barnes, Business and Technician Education Council, City and Guilds of London
     Institute, Royal Society of Arts
R J Hartles CBE, Association of Metropolitan Authorities
G Kendall, Training Commission
D G Libby, Department of Education and Science
J O Morris, Association of County Councils
L J Rees, Welsh Joint Education Committee
G M Rowarth, Association of Principles of Colleges, Association of Colleges for Further
     and Higher Education
B D Short, Her Majesty's Inspectorate
A F Warren, National Association of Teachers in Further and Higher Education

Observers
Dr F D Duffin, Department of Education, Northern Ireland
J Howgego, Scottish Education Department
R L James HMI, Welsh Office Education Department
P Watkins, School Curriculum Development Committee

Secretary
Geoff Stanton, Chief Officer, Further Education Unit

Objectives

The objects for which The Further Education Unit (FEU) is established are to promote, encourage and develop the efficient provision of further education in the United Kingdom and for that purpose:
a) to review and evaluate the range of existing further education curricula and programmes and to identify overlap, duplication, deficiencies and inconsistencies therein;
b) to determine priorities for action to improve the provision of further education and to make recommendations as to how such improvement can be effected;
c) to carry out studies in further education and to support investigations of and experimentation in, and the development of, further education curricula and to contribute to and assist in the evaluation of initiatives in further education;
d) to disseminate and publish information, and to assist in the dissemination and publication of information, about recommendations for and experiments and developments in further education.